LEVEL 5

Sherlock Holmes
& the Oxford murders

by

Rod Smith

João Henrique
Benfica

Richmond READERS

Richmond READERS

LEVEL 1

(500 headwords)

Maria's Dilemma
Oscar
Jack's Game
The Boy from Yesterday
The Black Mountain

LEVEL 2

(800 headwords)

Jason Causes Chaos
Craigen Castle Mystery
The Road through the Hills and other stories
Where's Mauriac?
Saturday Storm

LEVEL 3

(1200 headwords)

A Trip to the Stars
Dr Jekyll and Mr Hyde
The Canterville Ghost and Other Stories
Cold Feet
Frankenstein
P.R. and Prejudice

LEVEL 4

(1800 headwords)

A Trip to London
Dracula Jane Eyre
The Adventures of Tom Sawyer
Sense and Sensibility
A Floral Arrangement
Medical Match
William and Kate: A Royal Romance

LEVEL 5

(2600+ headwords)

Steve Jobs: the man behind Apple
Elizabeth II: The Diamond Queen

Contents

Introduction

CD1 1

The character of Sherlock Holmes

Sherlock Holmes, the world's most famous detective, was created by a Scottish doctor, Sir Arthur Conan Doyle. His first story, *A Study In Scarlet*, appeared inside a Christmas book in 1887, but the character of Sherlock Holmes did not become popular until after 1891, when that same story appeared in the *Strand Magazine,* a well-known London publication which was also sold in the United States. After that, the demand for Conan Doyle's stories grew so much that people queued from the early hours of the morning outside the *Strand Magazine's* offices whenever a new Sherlock Holmes adventure was published.

Conan Doyle based the character of Sherlock Holmes on an Edinburgh physician called Doctor Joseph Bell. The author first met Dr Bell in 1877, while he was studying medicine at the University of Edinburgh. Dr Bell was a professor at the university, where he gave lectures to students of medicine. Conan Doyle was immediately impressed with Professor Bell's ability to describe patients he had never met before from the way they behaved, the clothes they wore and signs on their body or clothing that indicated their habits or profession. From this method of 'deduction', Professor Bell was able to describe a person's character, occupation, and the signs of a particular disease with great accuracy.

By the end of his time at Edinburgh, Conan Doyle was working as Professor Bell's assistant. This gave him the opportunity to study his teacher's methods closely. He later used these in creating the character of Sherlock

Holmes. After the enormous success of the stories featuring Sherlock Holmes and his assistant, Doctor Watson, Conan Doyle wrote to his old professor with the words, "It is most certainly to you that I owe Sherlock Holmes".

There is, however, much more to Sherlock Holmes than his brilliant methods of deduction. His unhealthy habits, including the use of drugs, late-night visits to the rougher parts of London where he competed in boxing matches, and willingness to experiment on himself with various chemical substances, made him a unique and interesting character.

This individuality is even further emphasised when considering the emotional side of Sherlock Holmes' personality. He loved music and was fond of playing the violin; yet – with the one possible exception of Irene Adler in the story *A Scandal in Bohemia* – there is no mention of Holmes forming a romantic attachment to any woman.

This left the great detective with a mind almost entirely focused on logic, reasoning, observation and experimentation. There was simply no room for any of what Doctor Watson described as 'the softer passions'.

In many ways, this was tragic. For without something to occupy his rational mind, Sherlock Holmes at times appeared to be in danger of losing his mind altogether. For him, the greatest danger to sanity was boredom.

This made him a difficult person to live with, a demanding person to be with, but also one of the most memorable characters in the whole of fiction.

CD1 (2)

Oxford University and the education of women

For most of the nineteenth century, Oxford University was still a privileged institution of higher education reserved almost exclusively for men. This situation had existed for hundreds of years and it wasn't until 1877 that the university's professors were even allowed to marry.

By that time, things were changing fast. Many important people in society objected to the university's domination by the church; its focus on the classics, and its relative neglect of subjects like law, medicine, mathematics and the sciences. These objections, along with the growth of a modern industrial society, all helped to promote the idea of women's education.

In 1879 the idea became a reality, with the opening of Lady Margaret Hall. This was followed, later that same year, by Somerville College. By the end of the century, two more women's colleges had opened: St Hugh's in 1886 and St Hilda's in 1893.

However, despite the establishment of these four colleges, their female students were not allowed to take a degree. They could attend certain lectures, if accompanied by someone else, but they would be unable to gain a university qualification as a reward for their efforts.

It took a world war to change the terrible waste and unfairness of the university system. By 1919, as millions of men's lives were lost in battle and the important role women played both during and after the war was finally being recognised, the demand for equal rights to higher education could no longer be resisted. The following year, women were allowed to take university degrees.

It wasn't until 1974, though, that male colleges began to admit female students. Interestingly, the last college to admit members of the opposite sex was the women's college, St Hilda's, in 2008.

Today, every college in the university is open to both men and women. Eight hundred years of male domination have finally, and thankfully, come to an end.

CD1 3

The language of Sherlock Holmes

The spoken English used by Sherlock Holmes and Doctor Watson was a lot more formal than it is today. For example, a simple question like "Are you going to the concert with Annie?" would more likely have been expressed as, "Will you accompany Annie to the concert?" However, there were also less polite phrases used to express surprise, shock, or anger. Some of the most commonly-used expressions of the time that are used in the story are listed below together with their meanings.

Conversational phrases

Sherlock Holmes' Time:	**Today:**
At your service.	*I'd be glad to help you.*
Would you care to join me?	*Would you like a drink?*
Good heavens! (Or: *Good heavens, man!*)	*You can't be serious.*
On the contrary.	*That's not true.*
For heaven's sake!	*Stop doing (or saying) that!*
How on earth ..... ?	*That surprises me!*
Would you be so kind as to inform ...?	*Could you tell .... ?*

Words and expressions

the lower classes	*ordinary working people*
I intend to ...	*I'm going to ...*
I suspect ...	*I think .....*
My love is not returned.	*He or she doesn't love me.*
If you would allow me ...	*Will you let me ... ?*
... this good lady/man ...	*...this kind/helpful person ...*

Main characters in the story:

Mr Sherlock Holmes: the famous detective
Doctor John Watson: Sherlock Holmes' assistant
Douglas Crenshaw: lawyer & personal assistant to James McCray
Eleanor Taylor: a student at Beaufort Hall
William Taylor: an anthropologist* & adventurer; the father of Eleanor Taylor
Alice Taylor: William Taylor's wife & mother of Eleanor Taylor
James McCray: the disabled* son of Lord McCray & the brother of Alice Taylor
Lord McCray: a wealthy Scottish aristocrat* & father of Alice & James McCray
Annie Lawson: Eleanor Taylor's childhood friend & domestic servant at Beaufort Hall
Mrs Amelia Finch: Mr McCray's housekeeper & the aunt of Annie Lawson
Robert Lawson: Annie Lawson's father
Miss Constance Blake: the principal of Beaufort Hall
Chief Inspector Thomas Carson: the policeman in charge of the murder investigation
James & Millie Parker: brother and sister, and student friends of Eleanor Taylor's
Doctor Hamish Stuart: the McCray family doctor
Lorna Stuart: wife of Hamish Stuart & the McCray family nurse
Harry Walters: Beaufort Hall porter*
Jack Warman: Annie Lawson's sweetheart

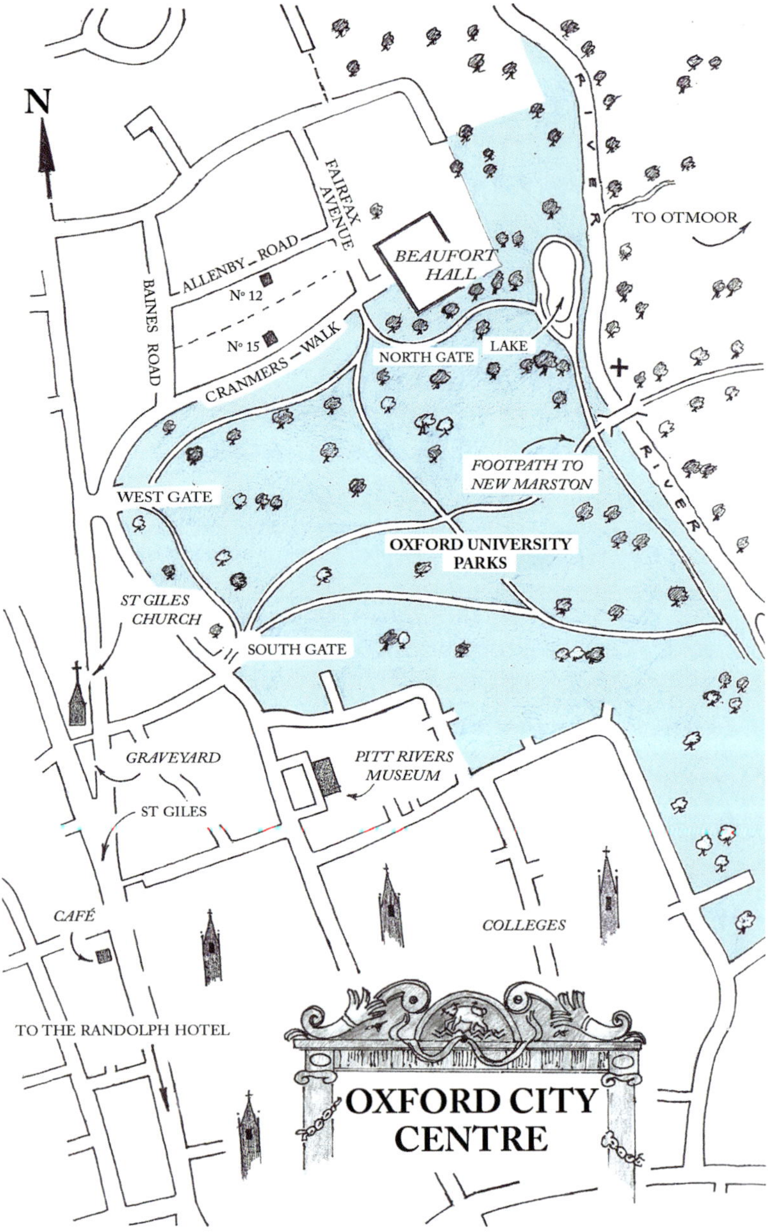
N
FAIRFAX AVENUE
ALLENBY ROAD
BEAUFORT HALL
No 12
No 15
BAINES ROAD
CRANMERS WALK
NORTH GATE
LAKE
RIVER
TO OTMOOR
FOOTPATH TO NEW MARSTON
WEST GATE
OXFORD UNIVERSITY PARKS
ST GILES CHURCH
SOUTH GATE
GRAVEYARD
PITT RIVERS MUSEUM
ST GILES
CAFÉ
COLLEGES
TO THE RANDOLPH HOTEL
OXFORD CITY CENTRE

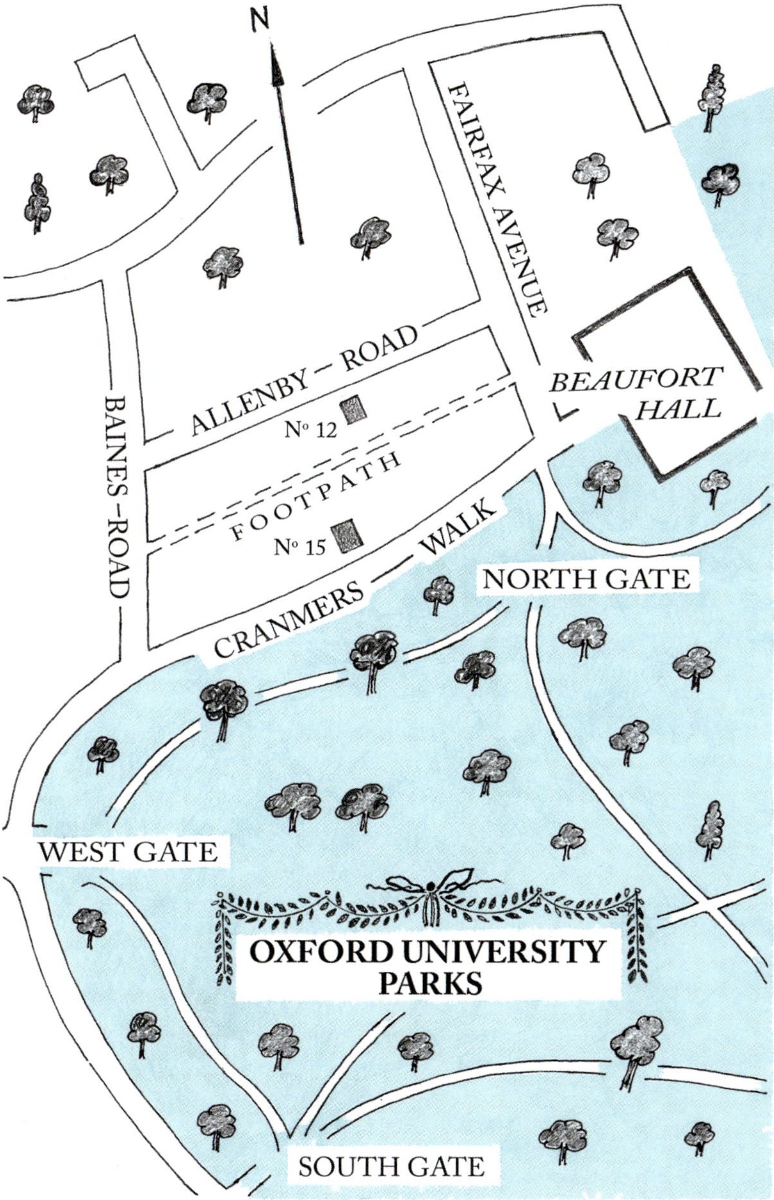
N
FAIRFAX AVENUE
ALLENBY – ROAD
BAINES – ROAD
No 12
FOOTPATH
No 15
CRANMERS – WALK
BEAUFORT HALL
NORTH GATE
WEST GATE
OXFORD UNIVERSITY PARKS
SOUTH GATE

Prologue

CD1

4

The evening of Friday, October 18th, 1912

The first murder had already happened. The second was only days away. The victim didn't know that, of course. She walked into her bedroom, turned on the light and closed the curtains – unaware of the man staring up at her from the darkness of the trees.

The man watched her shadow in the square of yellow light. He lowered his head, deep in thought. The plan was almost perfect. But there was still one big problem.

A church clock began to strike the hour. Seven o'clock, mid-October: dark, misty, and cold. There had still been some light when he entered the park from the bridge across the river. But no one ever saw him. If they did, he was gone so quickly they thought they'd imagined it.

Other clocks were sounding the hour. It was almost like a celebration. He was reminded of a group of boys he'd passed. They had been collecting money for Guy Fawkes Day[1]. In a little over two weeks, the skies of Oxford would be lit by a thousand fires.

It was then that the thought came to him. Yes, it could work! Suddenly, the 'big problem' seemed a lot smaller.

He looked up at the window one last time before turning back towards the river.

Then, silent as a ghost, he disappeared into the mist.

1 *Guy Fawkes Day is an English celebration of the discovery of a plan to blow up the Houses of Parliament in London on November 5th, 1605. In the days before the celebration, children traditionally collected money for fireworks★ to use around large fires in their family gardens.*

Chapter 1

A Disappearance

CD1 5

I had just finished lunch at the Langham Hotel when the man walked into the room. He appeared to be in a hurry and spoke urgently to one of the waiters. Both men looked in my direction. The first man gave thanks for the information and walked towards my table. I pushed my plate to one side, wondering what he wanted. Some medical emergency, perhaps? Or a message from Holmes?

It was neither of these things.

"Doctor Watson?" he enquired, laying a brown leather briefcase on the opposite chair. He was a small, thin man with fine blond hair and a rather nervous manner. I guessed his age to be around forty.

"★At your service," I replied. I stood up and we shook hands.

"Good afternoon, doctor. My name is Douglas Crenshaw. I hope I am not interrupting your lunch?" He spoke politely with an educated Scottish accent.

"Not at all, Mr Crenshaw. I had just finished when you arrived. Actually, I was about to order a drink. ★Would you care to join me?"

"Er … thank you, but no. I don't have much time, I'm afraid. I came up to London from Oxford and my train back leaves in just over an hour." He picked up the briefcase and we both sat down.

"Have you just arrived?" I asked.

"No, I came up last night."

"So, what do you think of the Langham?" I asked, spreading my hands proudly as I glanced at the walls of my favourite hotel.

Crenshaw didn't follow the invitation to admire our surroundings. "Actually, I didn't stay here," he replied. "I spent last night at the Bloomsbury Hotel, in Russell Square. I took an early morning walk through Regent's Park to call on Mr Sherlock Holmes. Unfortunately, he wasn't in. A lady, uh …"

"Mrs Hudson?"

"Yes, Mrs Hudson … your housekeeper*?"

"Landlady, actually, although she keeps house for us as well." I was beginning to feel excited. It sounded as if Crenshaw was about to offer us a case. We hadn't had one for some time. When this happens, Holmes gets bored and becomes very difficult to live with. My lunchtime escapes to the Langham Hotel were becoming expensive.

"Yes, well, Mrs Hudson told me that Mr Holmes was out, but that you were having lunch here. So I came right away."

"From your manner, I assume there's an urgent matter you wish to discuss."

"That's correct – there is." Crenshaw leant forward and glanced at the tables on either side of us, as if to make sure they were empty. "I am a lawyer by profession, Dr Watson. I am acting for *Walker & Alexander*, one of Edinburgh's top legal firms. They deal with the affairs of a Lord McCray of Oban, and his family."

"Oban – that's on the west coast of Scotland, isn't it? I visited the place once while I was a student at Edinburgh University."

Crenshaw smiled. "Then we have something in common, doctor. I, too, studied at Edinburgh, although in my case it was law, not medicine."

"So what has brought you down to Oxford?"

"I am to be married next spring. I am trying to save as much money as I can before I return to Edinburgh at the end of the year. My firm wanted someone to come down to Oxford to manage the legal and financial affairs of Lord McCray's granddaughter, Eleanor, until she turns twenty-one at the end of November. I immediately offered and was accepted; the position is a good one, offering more money and a living allowance. Eleanor is a student at Beaufort Hall. It's one of the new women's colleges in Oxford. I also act as personal assistant to Lord McCray's son, James. He is Eleanor's legal guardian★ but he was injured in a riding accident three years ago. He's now in a wheelchair★ and needs help in managing the family's affairs."

"What about Eleanor's parents? Do they live abroad?" I asked.

Crenshaw lowered his head. "No, they are both dead," he said, softly. I was shocked by the news but waited for him to continue. "Her father, William Taylor, died in Brazil and her mother in Oban, both within a few months of each other."

"A remarkable coincidence," I commented. "When did this happen?"

"Six years ago. It's a long story, but briefly…" He paused, as if gathering his thoughts, then continued, "Eleanor's father, William Taylor, taught Chemistry* at one of the Oxford colleges. Her mother, Alice – James McCray's sister – worked at the Pitt Rivers Museum in Oxford. She came down from Edinburgh to work under Professor Morley, who manages the museum and was also a close friend of William Taylor's. In fact, he introduced her to William and a short time later they were married. At times, it was rather a lonely marriage."

"Why was that?"

"Well, both William and Morley were particularly interested in the tribes* of the Amazon Rainforest: William, because he wanted to gain knowledge of the medicines and poisons they produced from the plants and animals of the region; and Morley, because he wanted to add to the museum's collection. Encouraged by the professor, William took more and more interest in anthropology. He'd always loved adventure and he eventually took time off teaching to travel to South America and make contact with some of the Amazonian tribes. Sadly, his final contact was an unfriendly one: he and his whole team were killed near the Peruvian border in the summer of 1906. Their remains* were discovered by a French expedition* late the following year."

"Did the news affect the health of his wife and lead to her own death?"

Crenshaw shook his head. "No. She died before her husband – while he was at sea on his way to Brazil. He was unaware of Alice's death before he died. It takes a long time for news from England to reach that part of the world. Perhaps, in the end, that was a good thing."

"Yes, perhaps," I agreed. "But if it wasn't grief that led to Alice's death, what was it?"

"Illness. Two years before William's death, she had insisted on joining him on one of his South American trips. That time it was to Paraguay. It was a fatal decision. While she was there, we think she was bitten by an insect and caught a fatal illness."

"And are the deaths of Eleanor's parents anything to do with the matter you wished to discuss with Sherlock Holmes?" I enquired.

"No, it concerns their daughter – Eleanor."

"In what way?"

Crenshaw looked down at the table. "She has disappeared."

"How? When?" I leant forward and stared at him.

He seemed unable to meet my eyes for longer than a couple of seconds. "The 'how' is a mystery, doctor," he continued. "The 'when' was three nights ago – Monday, October 21st, to be exact. Sometime during that night she was abducted★ from her rooms in Beaufort Hall."

"★Good heavens! Have you not contacted the police?"

"Er … no." Again, Crenshaw looked nervously down at the table. "You see, although James McCray and I are both sure that Eleanor was taken against her will, there's no evidence that a crime has been committed. Her rooms were quite tidy and there was no sign of a struggle. However, we think she may have been forced to cooperate under threat of violence, or given a drug of some kind which put her to sleep." I was about to object when Crenshaw stopped me by raising his hand. "But that's not the only reason we haven't contacted the police. Miss Constance Blake – the principal of Beaufort Hall – is anxious to avoid the bad publicity that Eleanor's disappearance would bring if this story reached the newspapers. There are many people in Oxford who oppose the education of women and would like to see places like Beaufort Hall fail. Unlike the older male colleges, they are all quite poor. If young ladies stopped coming because of any suggestion that they might be unsafe, the colleges could not survive."

"Even so, there must be another reason why Miss Blake has not gone to the police. After all, a girl's life may be in danger."

"Yes, you're right. Miss Blake believes that Eleanor was not abducted – rather that she just decided to leave college for reasons of her own."

"Could she not be right?"

Crenshaw shook his head. "No. Eleanor is a very ambitious student. This is her last year at Beaufort Hall. Her final exams are in the spring. It would make no sense for her to disappear at such an important time. To do so would threaten her whole future. The college has very strict rules. Even during the day, female students are not allowed out on their own. They must be accompanied*, either by another student or a member of the domestic staff. To leave in the middle of the night – and alone – would mean immediate dismissal from the college."

"Is there any reason to think anyone wishes her harm?"

Crenshaw shook his head. "Nothing definite, but James felt she had been rather worried lately. He could tell you more about that. Also, on the day before she disappeared, she had asked me to take her to church. She wanted to pray*, alone. She told me she needed God's strength during her final year of studies. But she didn't appear to be particularly worried. On the contrary, she came out of the church looking happy."

"Who discovered that Eleanor was missing?"

"Annie Lawson – she's the college servant who looks after Eleanor's rooms. But she's more than that. She and Eleanor were close friends. William Taylor knew Annie's father, Robert, who keeps horses out in Marston – a village just outside Oxford. William used to rent them from him when he and Eleanor went bird-watching* on Otmoor. It's an area of marshland* to the east of the city which attracts a lot of interesting water birds. Although Robert Lawson is poor, he is an educated man – self-educated, I believe – and he and William shared an interest in the natural world. William hired Robert's sister, Mrs Finch, to keep house for the family and look after Eleanor when she was a child; she's now Mr McCray's housekeeper, in fact. Anyway, Annie would often accompany* her aunt to the house and she and Eleanor became good friends. Later, Annie got a job at Beaufort Hall and the friendship continued.

"Annie discovered that Eleanor was missing at around half past six on Tuesday morning. She immediately contacted Miss Blake. Mr McCray was woken with the news a short time later."

"And now Mr McCray would like Sherlock Holmes to discover what happened to his niece before it becomes necessary to contact the police."

"Exactly. I realise we cannot expect him to leave his other obligations and come to Oxford with so little warning. Because of this, Mr McCray is prepared to pay well above Mr Holmes' normal fee."

I didn't mention that Holmes was bored out of his mind and had nothing to 'leave'. But not wishing to raise Crenshaw's hopes, I said, "I don't think extra payment will be necessary. The only thing that concerns Sherlock Holmes is whether or not the case interests him."

Crenshaw looked slightly disappointed as he handed me his employer's card. I read the address:

James McCray
12 Allenby Road
Oxford
Telephone: Oxford 311

Seeing that James McCray had a telephone, I was reminded of Holmes' attitude towards these relatively new machines. He hated them and said that their sound 'disturbed his thinking'. Even when I mentioned that a telephone might bring us a lot more cases he refused to change his mind. Still, at least Mrs Hudson had one we could use in case of an emergency.

Crenshaw stood up. "I must be going," he said. "Will you be returning to Baker Street, Doctor?"

"Yes," I answered, standing up and pushing in my chair. "If I'm lucky with a cab, I'll be back in ten minutes. I'm sure Holmes will have returned by then. What time do you expect to be back in Oxford?"

"Shortly after two o'clock. I'll report to Mr McCray and then go to my flat. It's 15A Cranmer's Walk, at the back of Allenby Road. Mr McCray is a man of regular habits. He's up by six every morning, always rests in the afternoon and is in bed by eight o'clock. His housekeeper, Mrs Finch, and I usually return to the house at five. If you could speak to Mr Holmes and call us with his decision sometime before a quarter past two this afternoon, it would be greatly appreciated. Also," he added, "there's a train that leaves for Oxford from Paddington station at a quarter past three. If Mr Holmes decides to accept the case, it would be a convenient one to catch. It gets into Oxford at around half past four. Mr McCray mentioned that half past five would be a good time to call on him. He will, of course, arrange accommodation for you both in the city."

❖

There was a cab waiting outside the hotel. Baker Street is on the way to Paddington, so we took it together. As we got in, I asked Crenshaw if Lord McCray knew of his granddaughter's disappearance.

"Lord McCray is an old man, and very ill," Crenshaw replied. "His mind is failing fast and he is not expected to live much longer. His son would rather not upset him unnecessarily."

"Is it possible that Eleanor decided to visit him before he dies?"

Crenshaw shook his head. "Without informing her uncle? Unlikely, Doctor."

CD1 6

Chapter 2

Conversation on a Train

When I returned to Baker Street, Holmes was lying on the sofa with his eyes half closed. An open newspaper was lying across his chest. He showed no sign of noticing that I'd entered the room. I hung up my coat and walked over to the sofa. "Glad you're back, Holmes. I've got news."

"So have I," he replied, pointing to the newspaper. "That's where I was – buying it."

"Very funny," I said.

"Our visitor's story must have been interesting – neither of you drank nor smoked."

"How do you know that?" I asked.

Holmes ignored the question. "Our visitor, Watson. Who was he?"

"His name is Crenshaw," I replied. "But you haven't answered my question, Holmes."

"The smell of whisky and tobacco soaks into your jacket like water on dry sand, Watson. But not today. So what does that suggest? I know the only thing that stops you enjoying your normal after-lunch habit of having a drink is if the person you're with refuses to join you. For some strange reason, you think it rude to do so. My conclusion? As well as being a liar, Crenshaw was obviously in a hurry and refused your offer of a drink. Since you rarely smoke without drinking, you gave up that pleasure as well."

This time Holmes had gone too far. "★Good heavens, man!" I exclaimed. "How can you possibly call Crenshaw a liar? I haven't yet told you what he had to say."

"You didn't need to for me to reach that conclusion. Anyway, what did he want?"

Still puzzled by Holmes' remarks, I told him the details of Crenshaw's story. Now that he'd called Crenshaw a liar, I was not hopeful that the case would interest him. In any case, most people who disappear return with a reasonable explanation after a day or so. But something about the missing student made me feel that there was more to this case than the facts alone suggested. Would Holmes agree?

At first I didn't think so, for the end of the account was met with silence. "Well, Holmes," I asked, growing impatient. "does the girl's disappearance interest you or not?"

"Not greatly."

I was surprised by the strength of my disappointment. "So should I inform Mr McCray that we will not be accepting the case?"

Holmes suddenly came to life. "★On the contrary, Watson," he said, jumping up from the sofa. "We are accepting it. Inform Mrs Hudson that we'll be staying in Oxford for two nights at least, probably longer."

Not for the first time, I found Holmes' behaviour contradictory. "I thought you said the girl's disappearance didn't interest you?"

"No, it does interest me. However, it is not the aspect of your story which I found most interesting. But more of that on the train, Watson. We must hurry. Tell Mrs Hudson what we're doing, then pack a suitcase. We'll meet back here in five minutes. Oh, and bring your gun. We may need it."

"Right." I suddenly felt uneasy. Holmes had sensed something in Crenshaw's story that I had missed: a danger to ourselves.

And he was nearly always right.

We arrived at Paddington station at 1:55pm. I wondered what the hurry was until Holmes told me that he wanted to catch the 2:05 train, not the one Crenshaw had advised.

"Why not?" I asked.

"Because I would like to look around Oxford first – if that's all right with you."

"Of course," I replied. Holmes was joking and I felt sure his real reason for arriving early was to surprise Crenshaw, whom he didn't trust. I suspected that this was also the reason he told me not to telephone McCray before 2:15 as I'd promised.

I bought the tickets and we found an empty compartment* towards the front of the train. Holmes sat by the window studying a map of Oxford which he'd brought with him. I wanted to ask him why he'd called Crenshaw a liar and what part of the man's story had interested him so much. I knew it would be a mistake to ask until he'd finished what he was doing; nothing annoys Holmes more than being interrupted in his thoughts.

So I leaned my head back against the seat and stared out of the window.

Dark houses with sad-looking gardens were gradually being replaced by green fields and winding streams. It started to rain and I suddenly felt tired. I closed my eyes and listened to the sound of train wheels and the rain beating against the glass.

I was woken by the ticket inspector, whose 'Tickets please!' sounded unnecessarily loud.

I sat up and handed the man our tickets, wondering how long I'd been asleep. He gave a sharp nod, handed our tickets back and left the compartment, closing the door hard behind him.

I looked across at Holmes. He was no longer studying the map. I now felt safe in satisfying my curiosity. "Tell me, Holmes. Why did you call Crenshaw a liar?"

He looked surprised, as if the answer should have been obvious. "Why did Crenshaw see you and not me?" he asked.

"Because you weren't in when he called."

"I went out for only a few minutes to buy the newspaper, as I normally do. You know that. Was it only coincidence that Crenshaw called at that exact time?"

"What else could it have been?"

"Look at the facts, Watson, some of which you don't know, I'll admit. For some reason, Crenshaw had to catch the 12:45 train back to Oxford. This didn't give him much time in London. Someone with so little time would have finished breakfast by around half past eight. They'd leave for Baker Street shortly after that, arriving no later than half past nine. But Crenshaw didn't 'arrive' until well after eleven o'clock – at the exact time that I had left our apartment to buy the newspaper. I was gone for no more than seven minutes. The chances of his visit and my absence occurring at the same time are well over twenty to one. Possible, but highly improbable. Add to that the facts you don't know. Mrs Hudson did tell him that I was out, but she also said that I would be no more than a few minutes and that he was welcome to wait. Crenshaw said he was in a hurry and chose to see you at the Langham Hotel. It makes no sense. Baker Street is much closer to Paddington, which he needed to reach before his train left at 12:45. Without question, Watson, the man was lying. He had no intention of seeing me. I believe he arrived well before he called and watched our apartment from the other side of the street. He saw you leave and continued to wait. He couldn't be sure that I would also leave so he was feeling increasingly nervous. He had to call, of course – his employer had instructed him to do so."

"But that's ridiculous. Why would he want to avoid you?"

"Because he knows something that he can't, or won't, tell us. I don't mean to offend you, Watson, but he felt safer hiding things from you than me. I am known as a keen observer of other people, someone who can identify their deeper motives. Crenshaw was afraid I would discover what those motives were. Did you not notice anything strange in his manner?"

"Yes," I admitted. "Perhaps you're right. He seemed rather nervous and rarely looked at me directly. But what were his motives?"

"That's what we need to discover," Holmes replied.

I was silent for a moment. I found the whole business very puzzling. Then I remembered my second question. "What part of Crenshaw's story did you find more interesting than Eleanor Taylor's disappearance?" I asked.

"None of it – only the questions you didn't ask."

I felt a little offended. I thought I'd handled the interview with Crenshaw rather well. "Such as?" I asked, roughly.

Holmes stared at the roof of the compartment and began to list the questions he thought I should have asked.

"Where was Eleanor when her mother died? Who was caring for Alice Taylor during her final illness? Why are none of William Taylor's relations mentioned in the story – parents, brothers, sisters, aunts, uncles ..."

"All right, all right," I said, holding up my hand to stop him listing every possible family relation.

Holmes took no notice. "Does James McCray live in the original home owned by the Taylors? If so, who owns it now – Eleanor? I looked at its position on the map. It's very close to Beaufort Hall. So why does she live in college and not in the family home? What subject is she studying? You mentioned that she has 'rooms' in the college. You know as well as I do that students, particularly in a poor college like Beaufort Hall, share rooms. But no mention was made of the person she shares her accommodation with. And why ..."

"*For heaven's sake, Holmes," I cried. "Crenshaw was in a hurry! I didn't have time to ask so many questions."

"That's good, because Crenshaw is not the man to ask – neither is McCray."

"So who is?"

"Mrs Finch, of course."

I fell silent, unsure whether or not Holmes was criticising the way I'd handled the interview with Crenshaw. As if reading my mind, he leant forward and tapped me on the knee. "You did well, Watson. I just need you to write down as accurately as you can the full details of your conversation with Crenshaw. Don't miss anything out, no matter how small."

"What, now?"

"If you wouldn't mind."

I noticed we were coming into Reading Station:

halfway to Oxford. I could only have been asleep for fifteen minutes or so. No wonder I still felt tired. I took out my notebook and forced myself to begin writing. I'm a fast writer, and it didn't take me long to finish the account.

I handed it to Holmes. He held up his hand. "Keep it for now," he said, then immediately changed the subject. "What do you know about Pitt Rivers?" he asked.

"The museum or the man?" I asked.

"Both."

"Not that much. Pitt Rivers was an army officer, wasn't he? Interested in anthropology and had the museum built and named after him as a place in which to keep his collection."

"You're right about the museum, not about the man. Mr Pitt Rivers' main interest was guns. At one time, he had one of the largest collections in the world."

"But the museum is mainly anthropological. It has ...."

"Yes," Holmes interrupted, "but it was only later that Pitt Rivers developed an interest in anthropology. Thanks to the work of people like William Taylor, the collection has grown enormously over the last twenty years or so."

"Did Pitt Rivers know Taylor?" I asked.

"I don't know," Holmes answered. "But Professor Morley did. Pitt Rivers gave his collection to the University of Oxford and Morley was responsible for making sure that the conditions of the gift were followed. There were three of them: first, the university had to provide a building large enough to contain the collection; second, it could only be used for exhibition, education, and research; and third, they had to employ people qualified to give talks on the items on display. Professor

Morley made sure it all happened."

"*How on earth do you know so much about all this?" I asked.

Holmes smiled. "Through reading your copies of *The Lancet*[2]. Really, Watson, you order the magazine but never seem to actually read it."

"That's not true," I replied, annoyed by the suggestion. "I read the parts that interest me, that's all."

Holmes laid a hand on my arm. "Don't be annoyed, old friend. I also read only what interests me. In my case it's usually articles on drugs, including poisons, and their effects on the body. Some of William Taylor's discoveries in this area were reported in the magazine. Following his death, they published an account of his life and work."

"Did they mention how he died?'

"Yes."

"And was it as Crenshaw described?'

"More or less. In the summer of 1906, Taylor led a small expedition into the heart of the Amazon. They were never seen again, but in the autumn of the following year a French expedition found the remains of their boat on the banks of a small Amazonian river in Brazil, not far from the Peruvian border. They also found human remains belonging to the members of the expedition."

"What did they think had happened?"

"There are many Indian tribes in that region who do not welcome contact with the rest of the world. For good reason," Holmes added. "They have no protection against the illnesses we consider harmless. The common cold, for example, can be fatal to them. It is reasonable to suppose

2 *The Lancet is a very old and famous British medical magazine.*

they were attacked to prevent contact with strangers."

"Surely the expedition had the ability to defend itself. Did they not carry guns?"

"They may have been taken by surprise. Attacked at night, for example, while everyone was asleep. If no one was awake to guard the boat, it's easy to imagine how the tragedy occurred."

As Holmes was speaking, I noticed that the train was slowing down. I looked out of the window and saw the famous Oxford skyline★ rising to the clouds. We were almost there. By now I was fully awake and anxious to begin the search for the missing girl.

Chapter 3

The Watcher in the Park

CD1 7

Holmes decided that we should leave our luggage at the station. One of us could come back for it once accommodation had been arranged. I knew 'one of us' meant me, but said nothing. We found a porter who took our suitcases and gave us a ticket to present on collection.

There was a line of cabs waiting outside the station. We missed the first and took the second. I checked my watch as we climbed in: half past three. We weren't due at McCray's for another two hours. I wondered what Holmes intended to do before then.

"Pitt Rivers Museum," he called to the driver, answering my question.

The journey took us past the busy shops in the city centre, then into the 'Broad' – a wide street full of pubs and ancient colleges. During the journey, Holmes sat reading the account I'd written of my interview with Douglas Crenshaw. I stared out at the Broad. It was full of students, some on bicycles, others walking. As we passed the King's Arms – a large pub at the far end of the street – a group of students came out of the main entrance. They were laughing and seemed to be having difficulty walking in a straight line. I was not surprised. Drunken students were not uncommon in Oxford. But something did surprise me: there were no young women anywhere. All the students I could see were men, even though there were now four women's colleges in the university. Beaufort Hall, the oldest, had existed for just over thirty years. Even the newest, St Frideswide's, had been around for well over fifteen. Perhaps Oxford's female students were too busy studying to enjoy the charms of the city, I thought to myself. If so, they might well be achieving better exam results than the men. I had no idea if this was true, but one thing was certain: a young lady out on her own in this city would be hard to miss. If Eleanor Taylor hadn't been abducted but had simply wished to disappear for reasons of her own, Oxford was not the best place in which to do it successfully. Perhaps with luck, and under the cover of darkness, she may have been able to leave the college without being seen. But then what? Her best move would have been to leave Oxford as quickly as possible. In London, for example, a young lady out shopping would hardly be noticed. So had she caught a train to London? Whatever the answer, one question remained: why would an intelligent girl with a bright future ahead of her choose to abandon her education?

No answer came to my mind. This forced me to consider the second, far more serious, possibility that Eleanor Taylor had been taken from her rooms against her will. Had she been put to sleep with some kind of drug, as Crenshaw suggested? Possible, but extremely difficult. Unless he had help, an abductor would have had to carry her out of the college on his own. A porter guarded the main gate so the only way of doing this would be over the college walls. Holmes and I would have to see the college before deciding how possible this was. Hopefully, McCray would be able to arrange this.

"Excellent account, Watson," Holmes said, handing back the notebook.

"Thank you, Holmes," I replied, and put it back in my pocket, before returning to my thoughts.

Despite my concern for Eleanor's safety, I felt more excited than anything else. It was always like this at the start of a new case. This made me want to arrive at McCray's as soon as possible and I thought Holmes' idea of visiting the museum a waste of time.

Holmes, on the other hand, had no sense of urgency about him at all. He sat beside me, calmly smoking his pipe. Rather than go straight to McCray's, he seemed content to spend an hour or so visiting a dusty old museum. I was beginning to wonder whether the only reason he'd agreed to come to Oxford was to examine Taylor's discoveries, when the cab suddenly stopped.

"Pitt Rivers Museum!" the driver called.

Holmes tipped the man generously, which produced a cheerful, "Enjoy your stay, gentlemen."

He left us standing in front of a large, not particularly beautiful, building. I was trying to decide whether it looked more like a church or a railway station when Holmes suddenly turned left and began walking away from it.

"Where are you going?" I cried, running to keep up. "I thought you wanted to visit the museum."

"No, the University Parks, Watson."

"Parks? You mean there's more than one?"

Holmes smiled. "Not really. It's just one very large park. Adding the 's' is just one of Oxford's many strange traditions."

"Well I'm an Edinburgh man, so I'll ignore the 's'."

"Very sensible, Watson. So will I."

The museum was now behind us and the entrance to the park lay a short distance ahead. The fields beyond were covered in mist and the light was beginning to fade.

"Is there any particular reason you wish to visit the park, Holmes?"

"Yes. On one side of it is the Pitt Rivers Museum and on the other, Beaufort Hall. I feel sure the three places are somehow connected to the mystery of Miss Taylor's disappearance. I'd like to view the whole scene before our meeting with McCray. If nothing else, it will give me a better idea of the problems a successful escape would have to overcome."

"Escape? So you think Eleanor Taylor wanted to run away from something? Or someone?"

"Not necessarily. She may have been forced to leave against her will. In that case, 'escape' would have been the wish of the criminal rather than the victim."

I remembered my earlier thoughts on the almost impossible task such a criminal – especially a male one – would face in attempting to remove an unwilling victim from an all-female college.

"Let us assume our criminal is a man," Holmes said, as if reading my mind. "Why would he have wanted Eleanor to leave the college at night, rather than during the day when getting out of Beaufort would have been a lot easier?"

"Easier, perhaps, but there would have been a lot more witnesses around."

"Exactly. Female students are not allowed out of the college unaccompanied. They have to leave in twos, through the main gate and past the porter who guards it. No, depending on the method chosen, leaving at night is the better plan. And remember, Watson, an abductor would not have to have been present at the scene in order to force Eleanor out of the college."

"Why not?"

"Blackmail. It works equally well at a distance."

Of course. Holmes was right. I hadn't considered that possibility. Feeling rather foolish, I fell silent and followed him into the park.

Holmes turned right and began walking down a long path. He told me it led to the River Cherwell. This formed a long border on the east side of the park. I felt as if I'd suddenly entered a different world. Mist was rolling towards us from the direction of the river. A row of trees stood like pale ghosts along the near bank. Everywhere was cold, damp, silent, and the recent activity of the city was now no more than a distant memory. I shivered. A feeling of loneliness ran through me as I tried to get used to these new surroundings. Gradually, sound returned. But it wasn't the careless laughter of drunken students or the rush of busy shoppers. All I could hear was the occasional call of a bird, the whisper of rustling leaves, and the sound of our footsteps on the damp earth. Feeling foolish at my sudden weakness, I looked away from the river.

We walked on past sports fields, tennis courts, and a low wooden building which looked deserted.

"Beaufort Hall is over there on the left," Holmes said, pointing to a large group of trees on the northern side of the park. The mist was thinner in that direction and I could just make out the shape of a roof rising above the trees. But instead of heading for the college, Holmes continued on towards the river.

As we got closer, I again felt a powerful sense of loneliness. But I now felt something else, too: fear. The river, mysterious and dark beneath the rising mist, seemed

to be a place of hidden danger. I told myself to be sensible and tried to imagine the scene in bright sunshine. I couldn't, and when we finally reached the end of the path I wanted to hurry Holmes on to McCray's as soon as possible.

Unaware of my unease, he had come to a stop on the near side of a wooden footbridge which seemed to lead to open country. He stared at the opposite bank for a few seconds, then began to cross the bridge.

I followed, unwillingly.

The mist was a little thinner on the far side. A narrow footpath led across an open field. Tall thistles* rose up on either side of it. I saw the dark shape of a cow moving towards us.

Holmes looked round as if he was about to say something. I didn't wait to hear what. I just turned and walked quickly back over the bridge, keen to get away from the place.

"What were you doing?" I asked as we reached the other side.

"Checking all the exits from the park," he replied. "But, of course, there's always the possibility of escaping by boat, especially on a misty night."

We turned right and followed a path beside the river that led to a small lake. Beaufort Hall was on its northern side. As we came closer, I got my first view of the college. It was a solid-looking building of red brick and white stone, four floors high, with an attractive clock tower in the middle. It was surrounded by a tall wooden fence. Getting the weight of a body over it would be almost impossible without help.

"I wonder on which floor Eleanor Taylor's room is?" I asked.

"A good question for McCray," Holmes answered.

He left the path and stood near the fence, looking up at the top floor of the college. Mist was rolling in from the river, breaking into strange shapes as it passed through the trees. I looked at the ground. It was a mix of mud and grass, wet from the recent rain. Holmes stood, deep in thought, then turned and looked back at the way we had come. Suddenly, he froze. He paused for a moment and then walked towards one of the trees. He stopped and knelt down beside it.

"What is it?" I asked, kneeling beside him.

Holmes examined the ground and spoke in a whisper, "We are not alone, Watson."

Chapter 4

CD2

1

The Photograph

Questions raced through my mind as we left the park. *Who was watching us, and why? Just a curious stranger or something more sinister★? And where are they now?*

We left the park by the north exit and came out into Cranmer's Walk. I recognised the name. This was the street where Crenshaw lived. The mist was much thinner here and we could see almost to the far end of the street to our left. The gates of Beaufort Hall were at the opposite end of the street. Just before them, on the left, was a sign which read *Fairfax Avenue*. I looked at my watch: we still had just under an hour before we were due at McCray's. As Holmes had prevented me from phoning from the station, I wondered if he still expected us.

Holmes checked his map. "Allenby Road is at the back of Cranmer's Walk. We can go this way." He put the map back in his pocket and I followed him into Fairfax Road. Allenby Road was halfway down on the left. Holmes suddenly turned and put his hand on my chest. "Let's take a look at Beaufort Hall first," he said. "McCray's probably still in bed."

When we reached Beaufort Hall, a laundry van was parked in front of the main gates. A strong-looking man with short grey hair was talking to the driver while a young boy carried baskets of clean laundry into the college. The grey-haired man looked at us suspiciously.

"The college porter," Holmes whispered and kept on walking. But there was nowhere to go. We seemed to be on a private road rather than a public street and there was no exit at the far end. Realising this, Holmes turned round. Feeling rather foolish, I followed, and sensed the porter's curious eyes staring at us the whole time.

Back in Cranmer's Walk, Holmes asked, "What was the number of the house where Crenshaw lives?"

I checked my notebook. "15A."

"A flat, then. Let's take a look."

We walked slowly past Number 15. Lights were on in the rooms on the upper floor. This was obviously where Crenshaw lived because some sort of building work appeared to be happening on the ground floor: there were no curtains on the windows, no furniture in any of the rooms, and a collection of builder's tools by the front door. We walked to the end of Cranmer's Walk and turned right into Baines Road. A few yards along, to our right, was a long, straight footpath. It ran between the backs of the houses on Cranmer's Walk and Allenby Road and came out into Fairfax Avenue. I checked my watch again: five minutes to four. Sunset was less than an hour away and it was growing darker by the minute.

Two figures – a man and a woman – suddenly appeared from the back of one of the houses on Cranmer's Walk. I recognised the man immediately.

"That's Crenshaw," I said.

"And the lady must be Mrs Finch," Holmes replied. No sooner had he said this than he called out, "Excuse me!"

The couple turned. As we moved closer, Crenshaw recognised me. "Doctor Watson," he said, nervously. "Er… we didn't expect you. You didn't call, so …"

"Yes, there was no opportunity," Holmes interrupted, sharply. Crenshaw's hand was on the gate of one of the back gardens. "Is this Mr McCray's property?" he asked.

"Er, yes, indeed," Crenshaw replied, and opened the gate. We followed him inside.

"We are a little early, Mr Crenshaw," said Holmes. "*Would you be so kind as to inform Mr McCray of our arrival? Please tell him that I will speak to him at the time he suggested. First, I would like to speak to...." Holmes looked at the woman. "Mrs Finch?"

"Yes, sir," she replied.

Holmes lowered his head. "Pleased to meet you, Madam. I would like to ask you a few questions if I may?" He turned to me without waiting for her reply. "Watson, if you would accompany Mr Crenshaw, *this good lady and I will be with you all shortly." He turned back to Mrs Finch and waved her in the direction of a wooden bench which stood in the middle of a large lawn covered in red and yellow leaves. As they both sat down, I followed Crenshaw into the house.

He seemed anxious and confused* as he led me into a library at the back of the house. He asked me if I would like some tea. I said yes, and he left me alone. He returned with the tea a few minutes later and said that Mr McCray would be down shortly. I drank the tea and waited. There was still no sign of Holmes. I went to the window and looked out at the garden. It was much darker now but I could just see Holmes and Mrs Finch sitting on the bench. She was talking and Holmes seemed to be concentrating on every word. I felt bored and wished they would come inside. Almost as if they had read my thoughts, they stood up from the bench and walked towards the house.

Holmes joined me in the library.

"What did you learn from Mrs Finch?" I asked.

"Amelia."

"What?"

"Her first name, Watson. It's Amelia."

"You must have learnt more than that, surely?"

Before Holmes could reply, Amelia Finch entered the room. "Mr McCray will see you now, gentlemen," she announced.

I looked at my watch. Exactly half past five. Crenshaw was right. Mr McCray was a man of regular habits.

Amelia Finch took us into a large room opposite the library. Two armchairs stood on either side of a coal* fire on the left side of the room. There was a long table beneath a line of windows looking onto the back garden opposite. A large man with red hair sat in a wheelchair at the far end, his legs and feet covered with a heavy blanket*. It was James McCray. His upper body looked fit and strong and I immediately felt sorry for him – he must have been an active man before his unfortunate accident. Crenshaw stood beside him. He was holding a large book of some kind. I noticed that his hand was shaking slightly. He led us through the introductions. McCray's welcoming, "Good afternoon," was firm enough, but he looked sad and rather lost.

Once the introductions had been made, I sat down. I expected Holmes to do the same, but he remained standing. McCray looked up at him. "I'm sure Doctor Watson here has given you the facts concerning Eleanor's disappearance," he began. "I am extremely worried. It simply makes no sense. For reasons your friend has probably explained, we have decided not to call in the police at this time. This means that, for now, you are our only hope, Mr Holmes. In any case, I have more confidence in your abilities than theirs. But, if you knew

Eleanor, I doubt that even your great abilities would be capable of understanding the reason for her disappearance."

"Without knowing her, Mr McCray," Holmes replied, moving towards him. "I can think of any number of reasons: pressure of work, a wish to pay a surprise visit to an old friend, a lover's arrangement..."

"You're not suggesting...?" McCray said angrily.

"Why not?" Holmes interrupted. "I would not be much of a detective if I did not consider all the possibilities, however unlikely they may seem. Your niece may be a model of all that is proper, but I know nothing of her character. It is for you to explain it to me."

McCray was silent for a moment before he spoke. "Please sit down, Mr Holmes. There is something I would like to show you."

Holmes sat down and waited. McCray turned to Crenshaw and nodded. Crenshaw placed the book he'd been holding on the table. As McCray opened it I saw that it was an album of some kind. It was full of photographs, papers, and what looked like old school certificates.

"The first thing you need to know is what Eleanor looks like," McCray said. He took out one of the photographs and pushed it across the table. "This is Eleanor. A recent picture – taken this summer." He leant forward and placed his finger on the middle of the photograph. "That's her, sitting in the centre of the group."

Holmes picked up the photograph and held it between us. I saw at once that Eleanor Taylor was a very beautiful young woman. She had long, light brown hair pulled back from her face and pale, shining eyes that could have been green or blue. She sat in the middle of the photograph, on the edge of a blanket spread under a tree. A group of young people – students, probably – sat in a half circle on either side of her. A young man on the far left of the picture was staring at her with a look I could only describe as somewhere between love and wonder. The remains of a picnic covered the rest of the blanket.

"Taken in University Parks," Holmes stated.

"Yes, it was," McCray replied.

"That building in the background, Watson," Holmes said, sensing my need for an explanation. "We passed it on the way here."

"Keep the picture," said McCray. "You'll need it for your enquiries. Return it to me when you're finished."

"Of course," said Holmes. He put the photograph in his jacket pocket and asked, "When did you last see Eleanor?"

"Last Sunday evening. She had dinner here."

"Who else was present at the time?"

"Just the three of us – Eleanor, Mr Crenshaw, and myself."

I looked at Crenshaw. He seemed uncomfortable. Our eyes met and he quickly looked away. I wondered what was bothering him. He turned to McCray and asked, "Will you be needing me any further, sir? Only, I have some matters to attend to in the kitchen."

"Very well," McCray replied. There was a hard edge to his voice. I sensed Crenshaw's relief as he left the room.

"How has your niece's mood been lately?" asked Holmes.

"Anxious."

"Have you any idea why?"

"Because of her studies – at least that's what I thought at first. She has important exams at the end of November. They are the last ones before her final exams in the spring. I asked her if anything was the matter but she said she was just a little tired."

"There was no problem with other students, her teachers or the college authorities?"

"Absolutely not," McCray said firmly. "Eleanor is an

excellent student. Always has been, as these school reports here will prove." He indicated the book on the table. "She's also popular with everyone at the college, and in the local community, too. Like her father before her, she does what she can to help the poor and believes that everyone has a right to a good education."

"Did this work interfere with her studies?"

"No. Eleanor was very well organised. She managed both her studies and social work very well. Lately, because of exams, her studies have taken up most of her time. She's been working extremely hard and is expected to do very well. It would make no sense for her to annoy Beaufort's principal, Miss Blake. The consequences of leaving the college without permission could be very serious. She knows that, which is why I think she may be in danger. The important thing is to find her as quickly as possible. If anyone can do it, you can, Mr Holmes. But if you have any success, however small, please report back to me at once. Say nothing to anyone else. This is a very sensitive matter."

"Yes, I understand," said Holmes. "But is there nothing else you can tell me about what was troubling her?"

"Well, I can't be certain, but I had the feeling that she had been contacted by someone recently. If this is true, then the contact must have been unwelcome in some way."

"Do you have any evidence for this?"

"No, it's just a feeling. I know my niece, Mr Holmes. Lately she'd been behaving as if she always had to meet someone and was late for the appointment."

Holmes nodded, took the photograph out of his pocket and laid it on the table. "What about the other people in this picture?" he asked. "Do you recognise any of them?"

"Well, that's Helen Richards," McCray replied, pointing at a black-haired girl to the right of Eleanor. "She and Eleanor share rooms in the college, but Helen is away at the moment – staying with her parents in Paris."

"When did she leave?" Holmes asked.

"At the end of last week," McCray replied.

"Before your niece disappeared?"

"Yes. There's also Millie Parker. She's the one who took the picture, so you can't see her, but her brother James is there." McCray laid a finger on the young man staring at Eleanor. "He's also an Oxford student. The others probably are, too, but I can't be sure. I've just seen them from time to time."

"Is there any possibility that Eleanor left to join Helen, in Paris?" I asked.

"If that was the case, she would not have left without informing both myself and the college," McCray replied. "Besides, there's the question of money. My niece receives a small allowance from her grandfather, Lord McCray. The payments are controlled by me and given to Eleanor on the fifteenth day of every month by my assistant, Crenshaw. This month's payment was due yesterday. Of course, Eleanor was not here to receive it. The amount is far too small to cover the cost of travelling to Paris. In any case, an attractive young woman such as Eleanor, travelling by train alone, would be remembered. Crenshaw has already made enquiries at the railway station. No one remembers a young woman travelling alone. Quite apart from all that, there's Miss Blake to consider. I'm quite sure that if she discovered that one of her students had travelled secretly to London alone, they would be forced to leave college. Eleanor would never take that risk."

Holmes changed the subject. "I understand that she was very fond of her grandfather. Did she visit him regularly?"

"She used to, twice a year, but not anymore. Sadly, my father's far too sick and is not expected to live much longer. Eleanor saw him in the summer. Everyone pretended it was a normal visit but really it was her final opportunity to say goodbye. She was very upset when she left. Shortly after that, my father's condition grew worse. The only person he seems to recognise now is his nurse."

The silence following this statement was uncomfortable.

"I have the feeling that the principal of Beaufort is a rather strict lady," I said, wishing to change the subject.

"She is," McCray replied. "Apart from not being allowed out of the college on their own, the students have to be back by six in the evening – unless there's a special reason, such as a visit from a family member."

"You live very close to the college, Mr McCray," Holmes said. "Could Eleanor not have lived here?"

"Another rule," McCray replied. "All students are required to live in the college."

Holmes nodded. "Who was the last person to see Eleanor before she disappeared?"

"Annie Lawson. She and Eleanor had gone into town and returned just before six."

Holmes was about to ask another question when there was a loud knock on the front door of the house. We heard the sound of Mrs Finch's footsteps, the front door opening and closing. It was followed by the sound of a woman crying.

Chapter 5

CD2 2

Sad Annie

Everyone left the room and went into the hall. Amelia Finch stood at the far end with her arms around a young girl. Crenshaw walked towards us. "It's Annie Lawson," he said, immediately destroying any hope that it might be Eleanor.

"Come into the kitchen, dear," I heard Amelia say. She led Annie through a door on the right. Holmes and the rest of us followed.

The two women sat facing each other in a far corner of the room. Annie was still crying. Her aunt passed her a handkerchief. The girl took it and held it against her eyes. Holmes was staring at her but she was too upset to notice.

I stepped forward. "Can I help in any way?" I asked.

The mixture of sympathy and professional concern in my voice drew a look of respect from Annie's aunt. "Thank you, doctor, but no. My niece is just very concerned about Miss Taylor. The two were very close, you see."

I heard the sound of McCray's wheelchair entering the room. Crenshaw went to help. All the activity seemed to have a calming effect on the girl. She stopped crying and made an effort to control herself.

"I understand you live in Marston village, Annie," Holmes said.

"That's right, sir," she replied.

"And do you walk to work from the village every morning?"

"Yes, sir."

"What time do you have to be at Beaufort Hall?"

"I start work at six, sir."

"What time do you finish?"

"Around midday, unless Eleanor wants me to accompany her into town."

"So if you have to return home at night, you surely don't walk back home alone?"

"Oh no, sir. I wait here for my brother. He works at the King's Arms, on Broad Street."

"I see. So that was the case on Monday night – the night Eleanor disappeared?"

"Yes, sir."

"As far as we know, you were the last person to see

Eleanor before she went missing. Can you tell me exactly what time that was?"

"A little after six o'clock – but I'm not sure exactly, sir."

"And the reason you stayed late that day is because Eleanor had asked you to accompany her into town, is that correct?"

"Yes, sir." I could see that Annie was beginning to feel uncomfortable. I felt sympathetic and thought it would be best if we left her alone.

"She wanted to go shopping?"

Annie hesitated slightly before replying. "Yes, sir."

Holmes leant forward. "What was Eleanor's real reason for going into town? Please tell the truth. It's very important that we find her."

Annie looked away and began to cry. "She h-had to collect a parcel. From the post office."

"Can you describe it?"

Annie shook her head. "It was large … and soft."

"Was the address of the person who sent it on the parcel?"

Annie shook her head. "No … just … a drawing."

"Did you see what was in the parcel?"

"No, sir. Eleanor opened it in her room. But before I left, she put one of her dresses in the empty parcel and gave it to me. It's at home. Tomorrow, I can bring it to work, but there's nothing on it to say where she is. She's just gone, and there's nothing…"

She began to cry again. "I'm sorry, gentlemen," said her aunt, "but my niece wishes to be alone. If you wish, we can leave the house…"

"That won't be necessary, Amelia," Holmes said. "I am sorry to have to ask these questions but we need to find Eleanor quickly. We'll leave you in peace now."

Holmes led the men out of the room. I was the last to leave and I closed the door softly behind me.

"What was that all about?" McCray asked roughly, once we were all gathered in the hall.

"Guilt," said Holmes.

"By God, if that girl knows something about Eleanor that she's not telling us, I'll have her dismissed from the college," McCray said angrily.

"I don't think she knows where Eleanor is, if that's what you mean," said Holmes. "The guilt is because of something entirely different."

"What do you mean?" McCray asked.

"It's not important and it won't help us find your niece," Holmes replied. "What is far more important is that we see Miss Blake and obtain permission to examine Eleanor's rooms."

McCray nodded. "That's all been arranged. I have made an appointment for you to see Miss Blake at nine o'clock tomorrow morning. I have also booked rooms for you both in the Randolph Hotel, just off St Giles'. The reservation is for two nights but I can arrange for you to stay longer if necessary. If you discover anything of importance tomorrow, please let me know."

"Of course," Holmes replied.

McCray looked at Crenshaw. It was a sign that our meeting had come to an end. Crenshaw opened the front door. We thanked them both and left the house.

CD2 3

Chapter 6

The Man in Black

"Did Amelia give you all that information about her niece?" I asked as soon as Crenshaw had closed the door.

"Most of it," Holmes replied. "But not the fact that Eleanor gave her one of her dresses in the empty parcel. It makes perfect sense because of the other things she told me."

"Which were?"

"That the two young women were very close – not only because they were childhood friends. You may have noticed that McCray used the words 'social' and 'studies' in the same sentence. It suggests that for Eleanor, helping people who were less fortunate in life was equally as important as her studies. I believe she helped Annie whenever she could, both emotionally and financially. And yet, I have a feeling the dress was something more than a gift."

"In what way?"

"For once, Watson, I have no idea."

We had reached the end of Allenby Road. It was now quite dark and the mist had thickened. We turned left into Baines Road. This would take us to St Giles' and the Randolph Hotel.

"You spent a long time with Annie's aunt, Holmes," I said, wishing to break the silence.

"Yes, time well spent, Watson. She managed to answer most of the questions you didn't have time for when you first met Crenshaw. For example, she was looking after Eleanor in Oxford at the time of her mother's death – in the house where McCray now lives. It's always been the Taylor's family home. It becomes Eleanor's when she reaches the age of twenty-one at the end of November.

"As you can imagine, Alice Taylor's death was a sad business. She had gone up to Oban to visit her father. Unfortunately, Lord McCray had to go to Edinburgh on business a few days after Alice arrived. It was while he was away that she fell ill. James McCray had been left in charge of things whilst his father was away. He immediately called the family doctor, Hamish Stuart. He brought his wife, Lorna, who is a nurse and is now looking after Lord McCray. Anyway, Doctor Stuart did all he could for Alice and left his wife to care for her. But Alice's condition grew worse – there was nothing anyone could do, it seems. Within a week, she was dead. Lord McCray didn't manage to get back until after she'd died and was terribly upset. After that, he focused all his attention on Eleanor and took a keen interest in her education. When news of William Taylor's death arrived, he sent James to live in Oxford. This was to make sure that William and Alice's wishes for their daughter to attend university would be followed. That might not have been the case if Eleanor had been left with her Aunt Edith, who strongly disagrees with the idea of women going to university."

"And now, even if we succeed in finding Eleanor, Lord McCray will probably not live to see those wishes come true," I said, "But tell me Holmes, why is he not in hospital?"

"Hates them, according to Amelia Finch. He's always preferred to be treated at home."

"So every time there's a health problem he calls in Dr Stuart?"

"Yes, but not anymore. And not only because he's too

ill to call anybody. Dr Stuart died in a climbing accident a couple of years ago."

"Good heavens! Bad luck seems to surround the McCray family."

Holmes had nothing to say in response and we walked on in silence. Just before entering St Giles', he turned right and took us through the graveyard* of a church. Again, I began to feel uneasy. Mist, silence, and increasing darkness were producing the same sense of fear I had experienced by the river earlier that afternoon. The bell of the church clock above our heads began to ring the hour: seven o'clock. It was now completely dark except for a faint, silvery light which hung in the mist. I sensed movement to my right and turned just in time to see a dark shape disappear into the trees.

"Holmes," I whispered, my heart beating fast. "I think we're being followed."

"Just walk on, Watson."

We came out of the graveyard. Holmes wanted to take one of the smaller streets ahead of us but I insisted on heading for the lights of St Giles'. For once, I had my way and we followed the trees that lined the centre of the wide double avenue. The entrance to St John's College was on our left. As I looked, the mist suddenly cleared and I saw a dark figure disappear behind the main gate. I froze, instantly. The figure I'd seen was tall and thin, yet there was speed and strength in its movements. The word 'deadly' came to mind. But there was something else about it that troubled me even more. The head appeared to have been covered entirely in black cloth.

It was as if it had no face.

CD2
4

Chapter 7

Murder

When we arrived back at the hotel, Holmes sent me to collect our luggage from the station, just as I'd known he would. I had some difficulty finding a cab so it took longer than I'd hoped. I guessed Holmes had fallen asleep before I returned because there was a 'do not disturb' sign on the handle of his door.

The next morning, I was woken by a loud knock on the door of my room. I looked at my watch. It was just after six o'clock. Feeling rather annoyed, I got out of bed and opened the door. Holmes was standing on the other side, looking impatient. Before I had a chance to say anything, he told me he wanted to get to Beaufort Hall early 'to observe the early morning routines' and asked that I meet him in the breakfast room in ten minutes. I agreed, impolitely, and went to get washed and dressed.

Half an hour later, we sat opposite each other having breakfast. Holmes picked up a local newspaper and read it quickly before passing it over to me. He sat drinking tea while I read the stories on the front page.

Anxious to clear the night's dark thoughts from my mind, I began to remark on some of the stories. "Oxford educates the highest levels of society," I commented, "but I see the lower levels are quite active here, too: thieves, robbers, murderers..."

"Those occupations are not limited to *the lower classes, Watson."

"Of course not. I just meant..."

"I know what you meant," Holmes replied, smiling.

"Violence has always been a part of life in Oxford. There's a great deal of bad feeling between the people of the university and those of the town. It's been that way for centuries." He stood up, indicating that it was time we left.

I folded the newspaper, feeling glad that I had been educated in Edinburgh.

❖

The sun had risen by the time we reached Beaufort Hall. Holmes had no intention of going inside so we sat on a bench near the entrance to the park and waited. I had no idea what for, and I felt sure that Holmes didn't either.

After a few minutes a horse and cart* rode past, heading in the direction of the college gates.

"That same cart passed us on St Giles'," said Holmes. "Follow me."

We reached a group of trees from which we could watch the college entrance without being seen. I wondered why exactly we were doing this, but Holmes wouldn't say.

The horse and cart had come to a stop outside the main gates. The driver – a rough-looking man who appeared to be in his late twenties – was directing a group of boys who were carrying boxes of fruit and vegetables into the college. The porter we'd seen the day before came out and handed the driver an envelope. After checking what was inside, the driver gave a brief nod and climbed back onto the cart, which was now empty. He gave a loud whistle and the boys hurried out of the main gates and jumped into the back of the cart.

"This way," Holmes whispered in my ear. I turned but he was already running into the park.

Despite having many habits I considered unhealthy, Holmes was extremely fit and I had trouble keeping up with him. We crossed the park and came out on the west side. I followed Holmes down a narrow side street which led into St Giles'. He suddenly turned, put a finger to his lips and pushed me against a wall. I heard the sound of a horse and cart approaching from the right; we stayed hidden as the cart we'd seen outside Beaufort Hall drove past the end of the street. There was little traffic at this time of the morning and it stopped in the middle of St Giles'. The boys in the back of the cart jumped off and gathered round the driver, who took some coins from his pocket and paid each of them in turn. They ran off in various directions and the driver drove away.

"I suspect the college porter and the man in charge of those boys have come to some kind of profitable arrangement," Holmes said, turning to me.

"What kind of arrangement?"

"Beaufort Hall is a new college. Those who run it don't have much experience. From what we've just seen, I believe the porter is using that to his advantage. No doubt he's charging the college far more than the cost of the goods. Remember you mentioned 'thieves' to me after looking at the newspaper I gave you this morning?"

"Yes, what of it?"

"I said 'looked at it' because you obviously didn't read it carefully enough. The article concerning thieves referred to fruit, vegetables and other foods stolen from a warehouse★ near the station. Most of the food wouldn't stay fresh for long so whoever stole it would have to sell it quickly. There would be nowhere better than a place like Beaufort Hall."

"And you think the college porter's responsible?"

"Not for the actual stealing, no. Just for buying the goods at a low price off the driver. Those boys make better thieves than either of the two men."

"So do you think this has anything to do with Eleanor's disappearance? Maybe she found out about it and was about to tell the college principal. If that was the case, the porter would lose his job."

"I doubt there's a connection," Holmes replied, "but it's given me an idea as to how Eleanor disappeared without being seen. First, we need to examine her rooms, so let's get back to the college."

At exactly nine o'clock we were called into the office of Miss Constance Blake, Principal of Beaufort Hall, as the sign on the door read. After the introductions were made, Miss Blake confirmed that Eleanor Taylor had not returned to the college during the night. She described the situation as 'becoming increasingly serious' and said she would be forced to contact the police if there was no news of Eleanor within the next twenty-four hours.

Miss Blake was a thoughtful, intelligent-looking woman. She smiled sadly as she described Eleanor as one of her best students – 'intelligent, hard-working and kind' were the words she used.

Holmes was more interested in knowing how the college was run than listening to a list of Eleanor's good qualities. To my embarrassment, he interrupted Miss Blake by asking detailed questions about the college. She didn't seem to mind and explained college life in detail: its rules, class times, daily study routine, and various social activities.

She confirmed what McCray had told us: Beaufort Hall was not a wealthy college. It could only afford to employ most domestic staff part–time. They worked from six to eleven o'clock every morning, except on weekends. Each of them cleaned, did laundry, and served meals for twelve students. There were sixty students who lived in five sets of six apartments located in different parts of the college. At weekends, the students were expected to look after themselves. The college's only full–time employees were the porter – an ex-army man called Harry Walters – and Mrs Bradshaw, the cook. She told us that Harry Walters was responsible for making sure all visitors to the college signed in when they arrived and out when they left. The only exceptions were the men who delivered food and supplies. However, none of these men came into the main part of the college as the passage leading to the storerooms was between Harry's office and the main gate. Harry lived in rooms behind his office.

Miss Blake also explained that when a new student arrived at Beaufort Hall, a list was made of all their possessions. She kept these lists in her office.

"What is the purpose of the lists?" I asked.

"I have always encouraged staff and students to think of themselves as part of one large family," Miss Blake replied. "Even so, we have had problems with stealing in the past – especially jewellery and clothing. That is why we have these lists. Occasionally, domestic staff have been accused of stealing items that were never brought into the college, so the lists also protect them from false accusations."

Holmes asked if we could have a look at Eleanor's rooms.

"Yes, of course," Miss Blake replied. "Normally I would ask Annie Lawson to show them to you, but she didn't arrive for work this morning – she is the helper responsible for Miss Taylor's rooms."

"Yes, we met her last night," I said.

Miss Blake didn't comment on this information and we followed her to Harry Walters' office, where she told him to give us the keys to Eleanor's apartment.

"One last question, Miss Blake," said Holmes. "Has the apartment been cleaned since Eleanor disappeared?"

"No, Mr Holmes. It hasn't been touched. I must leave you now. Please lock the door to the apartment when you've finished, and return the keys to Mr Walters."

"Certainly," Holmes replied.

After she'd gone, he turned to the porter. "When did you last see Miss Taylor on the day she disappeared?"

Walters replied as though he were being addressed by a superior officer. "Just before six o'clock in the evening, sir. I saw her go to her rooms with Annie Lawson."

"What was Miss Taylor wearing? Do you remember?"

"Yes sir. She wore a short black jacket over a long grey dress. She was also wearing black leather gloves. She usually dresses in those clothes when she goes to the city centre."

❖

The apartment Eleanor shared with Helen Richards was on the east side of the college. It was on the second floor and looked over the river Cherwell and the part of the park that Holmes and I had crossed the day before. The weather was unusually warm and the sun shone brightly through the windows. One of them was slightly open and a gentle breeze disturbed the curtains on either side. I could hear birds singing and the splash of oars on water as a group of students rowed a boat towards the city.

The apartment consisted of two small bedrooms and a shared sitting room. Two similar apartments were on the same floor with three more on the floor above. There was also a shared bathroom on each floor.

Completely tidy, I thought, as I looked around the living room. If Eleanor had been taken by force following some kind of struggle, then her abductor had cleared up well before leaving.

Holmes was on his hands and knees examining the floor. He picked something up from beneath a mirror on the far wall and put it in a small envelope.

"What's that?" I asked.

"A couple of hairs, light brown, probably Eleanor's. I'll need a microscope★ though, Watson. There should be a science room in the college. We'll ask."

It was then that we heard a woman's scream coming from the direction of the river. It lasted no more than a couple of seconds and was followed by an uneasy silence.

We went to the window. At first we could see nothing. But then, in the distance, on the far side of the river near where the footbridge crosses into Marston fields, we saw a small crowd gathering. A young man suddenly broke away from the group, crossed the footbridge and ran towards the city.

"My God, Holmes, what's going on?"

"We'll find out soon enough. Right now, I need to finish examining these rooms. I have the feeling there may not be another chance. Meanwhile, Watson, open that window and tell me if there's any way of climbing down to the ground without having to jump."

I raised the window and looked out. There was a drainpipe★ a couple of feet to the left. Because the

buildings were new, it looked in good condition and easily strong enough to take a person's weight.

I heard Holmes call out and turned back into the room. He was standing in the doorway of one of the bedrooms. "Take a look at this wardrobe in here, Watson. Tell me what you notice."

I went inside. The two doors of a wardrobe on the opposite wall stood open. A long coat and a number of dresses were hanging in a line on coat hangers*. One of them was empty. I commented on this.

"So what does that tell us?" Holmes asked.

"No black jacket and no grey dress," I replied. "So those must have been the items Eleanor was wearing when she disappeared."

"Excellent, Watson. Well, I think we're finished here. Now I need to find that microscope."

We locked the apartment door and went back down the stairs. I felt increasingly uneasy, unable to forget the dreadful scream we'd heard from the open window. A sense of anxiety seemed to fill the whole college: I heard quick footsteps and raised voices which grew louder the moment we reached the ground floor.

A young student came out of one of the rooms. She looked at us in surprise.

"Excuse me, Miss," Holmes said. "Could you tell us where the science room is?"

"It's on the ground floor next door, to the left," she said. "But do you have ….."

"Yes, Miss Blake has given her permission," Holmes interrupted, and we moved off quickly before the girl could ask any more questions.

Whatever was going on in the college worked in our favour. Any students who had been working in the science room had left to see what was happening, leaving us with the room to ourselves. Holmes found a microscope and began examining the hairs he'd found in Eleanor's apartment.

"Just as I thought," he said, putting the hairs back in the envelope.

"What?"

"Eleanor Taylor's hair has been cut, not pulled through brushing. It's been cut as short as a man's. I have little doubt that she did it herself."

"So she wanted to escape, and did so disguised as a man?"

"Not as a man, as a boy, Watson. Those boys we saw this morning delivering vegetables. They ran off in different directions so I doubt they all know each other. I also think the driver doesn't hire the same ones every day. He probably takes whoever he can pay the least money to. If that's the case, Eleanor could easily have escaped without being noticed by slipping in among them."

The noise coming from the quad had grown louder now so we decided to leave.

The sight before us as we stepped outside confirmed my worst fears. A very pale-faced Miss Blake was talking to two policemen, one wearing a hat and long brown coat and the other in uniform. The man in the coat was clearly a detective. Harry Walters stood at a respectful distance, looking serious. Female students were gathering round Miss Blake and the policemen.

We walked towards the group. Walters looked in our direction and met us halfway. "Terrible news, sir," he said, addressing Holmes. "One of the young women you were enquiring about has been found – dead. It appears she was murdered."

"My God! Eleanor!" I cried, unable to stop myself.

Walters looked at me and shook his head. "Oh no, sir. It wasn't Miss Taylor. It was Annie – Annie Lawson."

Chapter 8

CD2
5

The Secret Lover

The scene before us suddenly turned even more dramatic when a desperate-looking young man ran through the college gates yelling, *"Who is it?"*

A short girl with wavy red hair left the group surrounding Miss Blake and went to meet him. She took him by the shoulders and whispered something in his ear. This seemed to quieten the young man down, although he still looked distressed. I recognised him as the student in the picture who had been staring at Eleanor. The girl led him towards the main entrance, which was now unguarded.

"Come on, Watson – before they disappear."

By now the police detective was looking in our direction as if he wished to talk to us. But Holmes ignored him and raced after the disappearing couple. We followed them out of the main gate. They had turned left and were heading for the park. Holmes and I soon caught up with them. "Follow me," Holmes told them, "quickly, before the police call us back."

At first the couple looked shocked, but the urgency in Holmes' voice and his mention of the police made them obey without question. The four of us ran to the park and reached the safety of the trees.

Holmes pulled out the photograph McCray had given him. "I believe this is you," he said to the young man, pointing at the photograph.

The young man nodded, miserably.

"He's my brother," said the girl. "James Parker. And I'm

Millie. What do you want with us?"

"My name is Sherlock Holmes and this is my friend, Dr Watson. We'd just like to ask you a few questions, but somewhere quiet."

"I know a café not far from here," James replied. "It should be quiet at this time of day."

We followed him across St Giles'. The place he was referring to was on the far side, hidden behind some trees.

We went in, sat down, and ordered tea.

"I understand you're a student at Beaufort Hall," I said to Millie as the waitress finished serving us.

"Yes," she replied. "And James is at New College."

"How well did you know Eleanor Taylor?" Holmes asked, turning to James.

"Not as well as I would have liked," he replied.

"James is rather fond of Eleanor," said Millie, "but she doesn't allow many people to get close to her."

"Were you close to her?" Holmes asked.

"No. We were friends; Eleanor had a warm personality and was very considerate to other people. But she was also rather secretive. The two who knew her best were Helen Richards, who shares her apartment, and Annie... the girl who..."

"Yes, I understand," said Holmes. He turned back to James. "So 'fond of' really means that you're in love with Eleanor Taylor?"

"Yes, but *my love is not returned. She thinks of me as a friend, nothing more."

"But you've spent time together, alone?"

"With Annie's help, yes. Sometimes, I'd arrange to meet them in town. At other times we'd come here to this cafe. There's a garden at the back. Annie would sit there while

Eleanor and I talked. It was here that I told her I loved her. She replied that she was very fond of me, but not yet ready for love."

"When did this happen?" Holmes asked.

"Last month, after the picnic where the photograph was taken. I would have accepted what she told me, except..."

"Except what?" Holmes asked.

"Well, she was behaving a little strangely at the time. She seemed anxious and replied to my declaration of love in an absent manner. She wasn't focused, if you know what I mean."

"And you've no idea why?"

"I got the impression that she was frightened of someone. In fact, I may have seen him."

On hearing this, I leant forward. "What did he look like?" I asked, remembering the shadowy figure I'd seen the night before.

"It happened around the middle of last month," James replied. "Eleanor and I met a few times for afternoon tea, in various places in town. After about the third time, I began to feel uneasy. I couldn't think why. Eleanor seemed worried, but when I asked her if everything was all right, she told me it was. There was something else, though, which had nothing to do with Eleanor's mood. I began to feel as though we were being watched. Then, the next time we met, I felt sure I was right. We were having tea in the King's Arms. The place was busy, but I noticed a man who seemed familiar sitting in the corner of the room. It wasn't his face I recognised: he was in shadow and wore a hat so I couldn't see it. I think it was his clothes and something about the way he was sitting. I must have noticed him before without realising it. But this time, something happened that made me remember him. He was staring at Eleanor, hard. It was a cloudy day but every now and then the sun shone through the clouds. At one point the man leaned forward and just as he did so, the sunlight caught his face. It was a face you don't easily forget. The skin was dark and covered in tiny marks, as if it was diseased. His eyes shone like green fire. The effect was rather frightening and I had to look away. I didn't say anything to Eleanor at the time because I didn't want her to look round and attract the man's attention. But once we'd left, I told her I thought she was being followed and urged her to tell her uncle and the college about it. She just laughed and said I was being silly."

"Was that the last time you saw the man?" Holmes asked.

"No, there was one other occasion, and this time Eleanor's reaction was totally different. She, Annie, and myself were in town the week before last listening to a lunchtime concert in St Mary's Church. We'd just left and were making our way home along Turl Street when the same man suddenly appeared from behind the gateway of one of the colleges. I don't think he'd seen us – it was just a coincidence. Fortunately, Eleanor's uncle and Mr Crenshaw came into view at the end of the same street and the man disappeared. But I'll never forget the look of horror that came across Eleanor's face when she saw him. In spite of this, she denied that she was worried and said I was imagining things."

"Did Eleanor mention this to the college or her uncle?"

"No, and she told me to say nothing about it. That was the last time I saw her, but she wrote me a note saying we should see less of each other until the exams were over."

"But after Eleanor went missing," I asked. "Did you mention it then?"

"Millie didn't tell me that Eleanor had gone until yesterday. Even then, she thought there was some reasonable explanation. But now, with Annie's death, I must tell the police. I just wanted to speak to Millie first. That's why we left so quickly."

Millie suddenly turned to her brother. "James, I'm hungry. Could you find the waitress and order me a sandwich?"

James got up. There was no sign of the waitress so he went to look for her in the back room.

As soon as he'd gone, Millie leaned forward and grabbed my arm. "There's something important I need to tell you both," she whispered. "It's about Eleanor, and I don't quite know how to tell James.

"Last Sunday, around mid-afternoon, I was walking past St Giles' Church with my mother. She was taking me back to college. We saw Douglas Crenshaw walking around the graveyard, looking bored. My mother went up to speak to him. As they were talking, I looked inside the church. I came out immediately."

"Why?" I asked.

"Eleanor was in there – with a man. They had their arms around each other. Also, Mr Crenshaw had noticed that I was entering the church and called me back. I went over to him, trying not to look too shocked by what I'd seen. He explained that Eleanor had asked to be left alone to pray. I asked if she had gone into the church alone. He looked at me curiously and said, 'yes, of course'. He was clearly surprised by the question. I could tell that he knew nothing of the man inside the church."

"Did Eleanor or the man she was with see you?" I asked.

"No, she had her back to me and I could only see the top of the man's head. All I could tell was that he was tall with long, dark hair."

"How can you be sure it was Eleanor?" I asked.

"From her clothes, her hair, and the shape of her body; I know her too well to make a mistake. I think Mr Crenshaw truly believed she was alone, but Eleanor was taking a terrible risk. The things we do for love, doctor. And now I will have to tell James. It appears Eleanor has a secret lover."

Chapter 9

CD2 6

Watson's Account

Holmes and I left Millie to break the news to her brother. As far as I was concerned, the news was both good and bad: good, because if Eleanor had left college to join her secret lover he might be able to protect her from whoever threatened her; bad, because it probably meant the end of her university education. But we still couldn't ignore the possibility that she had been abducted before she'd had the chance to join the man she loved. I mentioned all this to Holmes as soon as we left the café.

"Let's just hope she's with her lover rather than anyone else," was Holmes' response.

"Do you believe Crenshaw knew nothing about the meeting?" I asked. "Or is it the reason he is acting so strangely?"

"'Yes', to the first question, and 'no' to the second, Watson. Crenshaw is the type of man who is used to receiving and following orders without question. He would lose his job if it was discovered that he knew Eleanor had disappeared with a lover. That's something he would never risk. He has too much to lose."

I hoped we might be going back to the hotel, but realised that Holmes was walking back in the direction of Beaufort Hall. I assumed he had decided to talk to the police inspector. Instead, he told me that he wanted to visit the Pitt Rivers Museum and talk to Professor Morley. I thought there were more important things we should be doing, but kept quiet.

In the end, it appeared to have been a wasted journey.

We were informed at the museum that Professor Morley had been teaching in the United States since September and would not be returning before the New Year. Since we were there, however, Holmes decided to have a look at William Taylor's collection.

It was in the south-east corner of the building and contained objects gathered from various Amazonian tribes. These included jewellery, clothing, cooking and hunting tools, and weapons. Of these, I found the hollow wooden 'blowpipes'* the most interesting. Some of them were several feet long. Beside them was a row of poison darts*. There were descriptions of the poisons used for these deadly objects and photographs of the plants and animals they came from.

We also saw a number of stuffed* birds in glass cases. Curiously, they were all water birds, but none of them came from the Amazon.

"These are British birds," I said, moving closer. "Not only that, they are quite common on Otmoor, where Taylor used to take his daughter bird-watching as a child." I felt pleased that, for once, I could give information to Holmes rather than the other way round.

It was now almost lunchtime and I was glad when Holmes suggested going back to the Randolph for lunch.

After lunch we met in Holmes' room. He had insisted on having wine with the meal and I was feeling rather sleepy. We sat in chairs on either side of the fire. I mentioned that we seemed to be making no progress in finding Eleanor. Holmes responded by telling me to go through the facts of the case so far, and to ask any questions that occurred to me along the way.

I took out my notebook, containing the account of my interview with Crenshaw, and began.

"A man called Douglas Crenshaw visits me. He avoids seeing you because he is hiding something – whatever this may be. After giving me some background information on Eleanor's family, he tells me that she disappeared under mysterious circumstances, and that her uncle is deeply concerned for her safety. He then returns to Oxford, hoping that you will agree to take on the case.

"You accept McCray's offer, but don't inform him immediately. We arrive in Oxford early to explore the area where Eleanor disappeared, hoping to get an idea of what difficulties either she or an abductor would have faced.

"Whilst doing this, you discover that we are being followed. It's misty, which is to the watcher's advantage, and he's skilled at remaining hidden."

"Excellent account so far, Watson."

I smiled and continued. "We arrive at McCray's and meet Crenshaw and Annie Lawson's aunt on the way. You talk to the aunt and get more information about Alice Taylor's death, and Eleanor's relationship with Lord McCray. You also find out that Eleanor has an aunt near Oxford who does not approve of her attending university. We then meet McCray, who shows us a photograph of Eleanor. She is a beautiful young woman with at least one male admirer – James Parker, whose sister, Millie, is also a student at Beaufort Hall. McCray describes his niece as ambitious, determined to pass her final exams, but she also enjoys helping the local poor. This makes her disappearance both puzzling and worrying: there seems to have been no reason for her to decide to leave her college so suddenly.

"During all this, Crenshaw is looking increasingly uneasy. Eventually, he finds an excuse to leave. What's he hiding, I wonder? Could he be blackmailing Eleanor? He certainly couldn't have abducted her – I can't imagine him abducting a kitten."

"He doesn't need to – he's got one already."

"★How on earth do you know that, Holmes?"

"His trousers, Watson. The cloth was slightly torn up and down both legs. The spaces between the tears were too small to have been made by a large cat, which wouldn't have behaved like that anyway."

"I see." Once again I was amazed at Holmes' ability to see things other people missed. "Anyway, what does Crenshaw feel so guilty about?"

"Wrong question, Watson. It's not guilt."

"What is it then?"

"Fear. Think about it. Crenshaw works for a respected Edinburgh law firm. He has a good position as McCray's personal assistant and Eleanor's financial manager. It's not a difficult job and he earns more money than he would back in Edinburgh – money he needs for his future life as a married man. Would he risk all that by involving himself in criminal activity?"

Holmes had a point. "No, I suppose not," I replied.

"So the question you should be asking is: *What is Crenshaw afraid of?* But anyway, I didn't mean to interrupt you. Please continue."

"Oh… right, uh… we then find out from Millie Parker that Eleanor has a secret lover. But is this enough to make her give up her education and abandon her family? Or was she abducted, or forced to disappear because someone was blackmailing her? Clearly, that's what we need to find out. The murder of Annie Lawson suggests that she is in great danger."

"So how does Annie fit into all this?" asked Holmes.

"I was coming to that. During our interview with McCray, Annie arrives at the house, unexpectedly. She's very upset. You question her and get further evidence of the closeness of her relationship with Eleanor. Eleanor helps her whenever she can; Annie's family are poor and Eleanor gives her gifts from time to time, including a dress on the day she disappeared. Annie also mentions seeing some kind of sign or drawing on the outside of the parcel that the dress was put in. Could that provide a clue as to where Eleanor is?"

"Perhaps, but I doubt we'll find it now," said Holmes.

"No, Annie's murderer probably took it. I assume that the parcel was sent to the post office for collection because Eleanor didn't want anyone besides Annie knowing about it – least of all Harry Walters, who seems to be aware of everything that goes on at Beaufort Hall. We also have reason to believe he's dishonest and probably wouldn't hesitate to blackmail someone if it was to his advantage."

"Let's go back to the dress that Eleanor gave Annie," said Holmes. "It was clearly more than a gift, Watson."

"What do you mean?"

"If – as the hairs I found in Eleanor's rooms indicate – Eleanor left college dressed as a boy, where did the boys' clothing come from?"

I suddenly realised the importance of what Holmes was saying. "Of course – whoever sent the parcel had put a set of boy's clothing inside it. Eleanor then gave Annie her dress..."

"Not just the dress, Watson," Holmes interrupted, "but everything she was wearing that day."

"Of course, so people would assume that was what she was wearing and make it more difficult to find her. She probably told Annie to say nothing about it, but after Eleanor had been gone for a few days she became worried. Do you think she knew that Eleanor intended to disappear with her lover?"

"I don't believe so, but continue with your account, Watson."

"There's not much more to say," I replied. "It seems clear to me that Eleanor's secret lover sent her the boys' clothes to help her escape, along with some sort of sign on the outside of the parcel which only they knew the meaning of. It could have referred to a meeting place, for example. Using a sign like that was easier, quicker and safer than writing a note and putting it inside the parcel. But is it possible that Annie's murderer also knew what the sign meant? Did he murder her in order to get hold of the parcel? If this is true, we need to find Eleanor quickly before she becomes his second victim."

"Yes, we do," Holmes replied. He stood up and laid his hand on my shoulder. "Excellent account, Watson. No wonder your stories of our adventures are so popular."

"Thank you, Holmes," I replied, feeling pleased.

"It's wrong, of course. Almost entirely wrong."

Chapter 10

A Second Disappearance

CD3 1

Before I had a chance to respond to Holmes' astonishing remark, there was a loud knock at the door. It swung open and we saw a man in a hat and brown coat staring at us from the doorway. I recognised him immediately: it was the police inspector we had seen earlier at Beaufort Hall.

"Found you at last, Mr Holmes," he said, stepping into the room.

Holmes stood up and shook his hand. "Chief Inspector Carson," the man said.

"Pleased to meet you, inspector," Holmes replied. I noticed that he was looking anything but pleased. "This gentleman here is my friend, Dr Watson."

Carson gave me a brief nod and turned back to Holmes. "I wanted to speak to you earlier, Mr Holmes, but you and Dr Watson here left Beaufort Hall before I got the chance." He smiled, but there was annoyance in his voice. "However, we've been busy – and lucky."

"Oh?" Holmes replied.

"Yes. I have been informed of your investigation into what appears to be the disappearance of a young lady called Eleanor Taylor on the night of Monday, October 21st."

"Correct," said Holmes.

Carson looked serious. "This is a matter that should have been reported to the police."

"At first, no crime was suspected, Inspector," Holmes replied. "It was thought that Eleanor had decided to leave college but would return before long."

"She didn't though, did she? Look, I know of your reputation, Mr Holmes, but not every crime has to be complicated." Carson was looking pleased with himself, and we were about to find out why. "You might like to know that we have just charged a man with the murder of Annie Lawson. He may also be able to give us information concerning Eleanor Taylor."

"Who have you charged?" Holmes asked.

"Name's Jack Warman, a former sweetheart of Miss Lawson's. Their relationship ended a week before Miss Taylor disappeared."

"Has he admitted to the crime?" Holmes asked.

Carson smiled unpleasantly. "Not yet. But he will."

"And how was she killed?"

"Strangled*. By a strong man with large hands, probably wearing gloves."

"And what evidence do you have that Warman is the murderer?"

"After Warman and Miss Lawson broke up, several witnesses heard him boasting in a pub that he'd kill Annie for leaving him. He also threatened to teach Eleanor Taylor a lesson – he thought she'd convinced Miss Lawson to leave him. Warman had no alibi* for the time of the murder, which took place sometime between half past four and half past six in the morning. Also, his clothes and gloves were covered in the same plant material that grows in the field where Miss Lawson's body was found. Warman's a large, strong man, perfectly capable of committing the crime. I believe that further questioning will lead us to Eleanor Taylor. I only hope we're not too late."

"I congratulate you, Chief Inspector," said Holmes, "and wish you all the best in finding Miss Taylor alive and well."

"I take it, then, that your investigation will end?"

"Not until Mr McCray informs us that he no longer needs our help."

Carson looked disappointed. "I see," he said. "Well, just remember not to interfere with our enquiries – any more than you already have," he added, looking hard at Holmes. "I heard from Miss Blake that you examined Eleanor Taylor's rooms."

Holmes nodded.

"Well? Did you find anything?"

"Only a few hairs – belonging to Eleanor, I believe."

"Hmm," Carson muttered, as if this was unimportant. He didn't bother to ask Holmes if he'd kept any of them. "I will need both your fingerprints*, gentlemen, so I don't have to consider them with any others we may find in the apartment. A cab is waiting outside to take us to the police station."

We followed Carson down the stairs. "Not the friendliest of policemen," I whispered to Holmes as we went.

"Sometimes it's better that way," Holmes answered. "The friendly ones are worse. They get in the way of an investigation, hoping to take the credit for whatever we manage to find out. Since Carson believes he's found out quite a lot already, he'll probably leave us alone."

I felt exhausted and almost fell asleep during the cab ride to the police station. Even my curiosity concerning Holmes' remark that my account was 'wrong' was failing to keep me awake.

On arrival, Holmes asked Carson if they had taken a photograph of Warman.

"Of course," he replied. "That's one of the first things we do."

"May I see it?"

The inspector went to a desk at the back of the reception area and came back with a large brown file. Meanwhile, a friendlier sergeant called George Hobbes was taking our fingerprints. When he'd finished, Carson took out the photograph and laid it on the counter in front of us.

We recognised the man immediately. It was the driver of the horse and cart we'd seen outside Beaufort Hall early that morning.

"Do you know this man?" Carson asked suspiciously, seeing the look of surprise on my face.

"No," I lied.

"But we'd like to speak to him," Holmes added.

"I don't think that will be necessary. You can leave the interviewing to us."

"*If you would allow me to speak with him, his confession may come sooner rather than later."

Carson considered this possibility. If it was true, then he would undoubtedly take the credit. "Very well," he said. "Fifteen minutes, no more."

"Thank you, Inspector. Is he here?"

"No, he's in Oxford Prison. It's next to the old castle. I'll take you there now."

Holmes turned to me. "You look tired, Watson. Take a cab back to the hotel. I'll meet you later."

I was only too glad to get away. I found a cab and was back at the Randolph soon after. I went up to my room and lay on the bed. Within minutes, I'd fallen into a deep sleep.

It was still light when I woke up. I looked at my watch: almost eight o'clock. 'It should be dark by now', was my first thought. Slowly, I realised what had happened: it was five minutes to eight in the morning, not the evening. I had slept, fully dressed, for over sixteen hours.

Rubbing my eyes, I went to take a bath. Twenty minutes later I was clean, wide awake, and dressed in a fresh set of clothes. Breakfast was served until nine o'clock so I went to call Holmes, anxious to ask about his interview with Jack Warman, and to find out why his view of the case was so different from mine. But as I went towards the door of my room, I noticed that a note had been pushed underneath it. Curious, I bent down and picked it up. It was from Holmes, and read:

> Didn't want to wake you, Watson. This is to let you know that I will be away for the next few days. If all goes well, I will be back Sunday evening. In the meantime, see what you can find out from Crenshaw. *Did you notice the position of the back windows of his flat? They give a perfect view of 12 Allenby Road – especially at this time of year. Interesting. Also, get a complete list from Amelia Finch of every person who has visited the house over the past month.*
>
> Thank you, and take care, my friend.
>
> Holmes

What on earth did Holmes mean about the back

windows of Crenshaw's flat? I was too annoyed to spend time puzzling over it. The list made more sense but I couldn't think of such things right now. I felt abandoned and not trusted. Why hadn't Holmes mentioned where and why he was going?

Chapter 11

The Hidden Paper

CD3
2

I calmed down over breakfast. After all, Holmes may have explained his theories regarding the case if Carson hadn't appeared when he did. Also, on closer examination of his note, I realised that 'a few days' may only be two if 'all went well'. I hoped it would be no longer. Nevertheless, his sudden disappearance in the middle of a case might not be easy to explain to Mr McCray. I decided to call on him after breakfast when Crenshaw might also be there. Perhaps I could discover what he was hiding and work out what Holmes was referring to in his note.

After breakfast, I spent some time reading a newspaper account of the murder of Annie Lawson. Apart from the phrase, 'a man is helping police with their enquiries', there was no mention of Jack Warman.

I left the hotel at half past ten. It was a warm, sunny morning, much like the day before. All signs of the mist that had filled the city since we'd arrived had disappeared. It was a perfect day for a walk so I decided to stroll through the University Park.

Unlike my previous visits, the park was full of students. Some sat leaning against trees and reading; others were walking along the river. Two policemen stood on the far side of the park in the area where Annie's body had been found, and which was now closed to the public.

An idea suddenly occurred to me. If Annie had been murdered because her murderer didn't want the address to be found, it might be worth visiting her father. I had no idea where in Marston he lived but decided that the horse-riding stables* he owned shouldn't be too hard to find.

There was no doubt that the police had been there already. But since Carson believed he had caught Annie's murderer, they may not have searched the place very thoroughly. If Annie knew more than she'd told us, she may have recorded it somewhere. It was worth looking – if her father gave me his permission.

The prospect of visiting a man who had just lost his daughter was not one I was looking forward to. However, being a doctor, I had more experience than most in dealing with situations involving loss. I made my way over the footbridge, trying to ignore the suspicious looks of the two policemen as I reached the far side of the river, where I had felt so uneasy on my first visit to the park with Holmes.

Finding Annie's house was even easier than I'd expected. As I reached the edge of the village, a line of horse riders came out of a gate on my right. A sign above it read 'Horses for Hire'. The riders rode away from the city and I looked in the direction they'd come from. At the end of a long track, a woman was closing some stable doors. She seemed familiar, and as I got closer I recognised her – Amelia Finch, Annie's aunt. I assumed McCray had given her the day off to be with her brother.

"Dr Watson," she said, looking pale and sad as I approached. "I didn't expect to see you here, sir."

"No, and I'm sorry to trouble you and your brother at such a terrible time. I can only offer my deepest sympathies, although words can offer little comfort."

"We thank you, sir. Did you wish to see Annie's father?"

"Yes, if that is at all possible. But first there is something I need from you." She looked puzzled and waited for me to continue. "This may seem strange, and perhaps unwelcome at this difficult time, but I need a list of all the people you can remember visiting Mr McCray's house over the past month."

"Whatever for?"

"It is a request from Sherlock Holmes. He had to leave Oxford rather suddenly for a few days."

"I see. Well, it shouldn't be that difficult. Mr McCray rarely has visitors." As she spoke, I took out my notebook. "Let's see. Eleanor – and Annie, of course. Myself and Mr Crenshaw. My husband, John Finch, to pick me up from work a few times. Eleanor's aunt Edith – twice, I believe .... oh, and Jack Warman came calling for Annie on one occasion. Damn the man!" I looked at her in sympathy. "The postman, coalman*, milkman*. Jason Hicks, once a week – he's the gardener. Some friends of Eleanor's: Helen Richards, Millie and James Parker and a few others whose names I don't know, I'm afraid."

"Were they all students?"

"I believe so, although I can't be sure. And that's about it. I can't remember anyone else. Mr McCray may have seen someone when I wasn't there, of course. On a Sunday, perhaps, but probably not during the week because he goes to bed just after I leave at eight o'clock in the evening."

I finished writing, closed the notebook, and thanked her.

"Would you like to see my brother now, Doctor?"

"Yes, if it's not too much trouble. There are just a few questions I'd like to ask him."

"I'm sure he's told the police all he knows. They interviewed him yesterday."

"I realise that," I replied. "But they may have missed something. You see, Mr Holmes and I believe Annie's death is connected to Eleanor's disappearance. This means that her life may be in danger, too. Annie may have mentioned something to her father which might indicate where Eleanor is."

"I doubt you'll get much out of Robert at the moment. He's terribly upset; we both are. But you can try. Follow me."

I followed her to a small cottage behind the stables. We walked around the side and into a back garden. Robert Lawson was sitting on a garden bench in front of an old wooden table, staring at a line of distant trees.

"Dr Watson's here to see you, Robert," his sister announced. She laid a hand on his shoulder. "I'll be back in a few minutes with some tea." She turned, gave me a sad smile and went into the cottage.

"I'm so sorry to trouble you at a time like this, Mr Lawson," I said, standing uncomfortably.

"Take a seat." He moved to make room on the bench. "My sister told me that you and Mr Sherlock Holmes are investigating the disappearance of Eleanor Taylor. I imagine your wish to see me is somehow connected to that." Lawson spoke like an educated man, just as Crenshaw had described.

"That's correct," I replied.

"Eleanor was very good to Annie and our family. Now they're both gone. I'll help in any way I can, but I don't see how. The police are holding Jack Warman for the murder of my daughter. If he's capable of such a crime he may have killed Eleanor, too. But the police will make him talk. I don't see what anyone else can do."

I could see that Lawson was convinced that Warman had killed his daughter. It would be foolish to anger him by questioning this belief, so I said, "Warman may have an accomplice who is holding Eleanor somewhere. That person could be equally dangerous. For that reason, any information at all you can give me may help."

"What kind of information? Annie was more upset than anyone about Eleanor's disappearance. She had no idea what had happened."

"I'm sure Annie knew nothing about Eleanor's disappearance. But Eleanor's uncle said she'd been worried for some days before she went missing. He thought it was because someone she was frightened of had contacted her. She may have said something to Annie which she later mentioned to you."

Lawson shook his head. "No, nothing at all. The police asked me that question and I told them the same thing."

Mrs Finch returned with the tea. I was glad she was back. Somehow it made what I was about to ask easier. I stood up and insisted she take my seat. She thanked me, and as she was pouring the tea I asked, "Would you mind if I had a look at Annie's room, Mr Lawson? It's just that Eleanor may have given her something which might provide a clue to where she is."

Lawson looked as if he was about to object, but his sister spoke first. "I don't think there's any harm in that, do you, Robert? The police have examined her room already, so I don't think you'll find anything, but you may as well have a look while you're here. It's the room on the left at the top of the stairs. Apart from whatever the police found, it hasn't been touched since the morning she left."

I thanked them and made my way to the back door of the cottage.

Annie's room was small, narrow and tidy. The bed had been made and every surface appeared to be free of dust. I looked under the bed. Nothing. I pulled back the sheets and checked under the pillows. Still nothing. Next to the bed was a small table with a single drawer. I opened it. Inside, there was a hand mirror, a hairbrush, and some ribbons. I closed the drawer and looked at the wall opposite. There was a shelf on the left side. It displayed family photographs and a book on British birds. I opened the book and saw that it was full of beautiful pictures, but no important piece of paper fell out when I shook it. Next to the shelf there was a wardrobe. This seemed to be the only place where I might find something.

I opened the doors and looked inside. The clothes, which were plain and well looked after, were all on hangers. There was no sign of anything that looked like it had belonged to Eleanor. Nevertheless, I checked any item that had pockets. There was nothing inside any of them. Disappointed, I turned around and took one last look around the room. I was about to leave when I thought I might as well check under the mattress. I lifted it, expecting to find nothing there. But to my surprise, a newspaper lay beneath it. It was a copy of the *Oxford Mail*. I looked at the date on its front page: October 21st – the day Eleanor disappeared. Why had Annie kept that day's paper? I looked inside it. There was nothing but local news. I folded the paper and put it in the inside pocket of my jacket. I couldn't understand why Annie had wanted to hide it, but thought Holmes might be able to make something of it.

I closed the door behind me and made my way back downstairs.

Robert Lawson and his sister were still drinking tea. I joined them and, feeling rather guilty, said I'd found nothing. As soon as I'd finished my tea, I thanked them both and left.

I walked slowly back towards Oxford. My visit seemed to have achieved nothing. I would have a closer look at the newspaper when I returned to the hotel, but at the moment it made no sense. I decided to visit McCray later in the afternoon.

My thoughts turned to Holmes. 'Where on earth has he gone?' I wondered. It wasn't the first time he'd disappeared without any explanation. I began to feel annoyed again, but the warmth of the afternoon sun on my face soon improved my mood.

Back at the hotel, I lay on the bed and took a closer look at the newspaper. None of the stories appeared to have any connection with either Eleanor's disappearance or Annie's murder. I was about to put the paper away when I noticed some pencil drawings on the side of the back page. They were simple drawings of birds in flight. Had Annie copied them from the drawing on the parcel? I could think of no other possible connection with Eleanor. In any case, they were meaningless to me. Maybe not to Holmes, though. I would show them to him when he returned. I put the paper to one side, closed my eyes, and fell asleep.

Chapter 12

CD3
3

The Body in the Attic

It was dark by the time I woke up. I looked at my watch: five past seven. I'd overslept* again and it was too late to visit McCray. But what about Crenshaw? He'd probably be home by now. I decided to pay him a visit instead.

For some reason I wasn't hungry, so I got dressed and left the hotel without having anything to eat. Outside it was windy, but the night was clear and full of stars.

I arrived at Crenshaw's at twenty to eight and walked straight up to the front door. No lights were on in any of the upstairs rooms at the front of the house. I hoped Crenshaw was in one of the rooms at the back. There appeared to be no bell beside the front door so I turned the handle. The door swung open and I stepped inside.

It was completely dark in the hall. I felt for a light switch but couldn't find one, so I waited for my eyes to get used to the darkness. Gradually, I saw the shape of a stairway ahead, lit by the light of the moon coming through a window somewhere above. I made my way towards the stairs, thinking that Crenshaw could still be at McCray's and might be back at any moment.

The light improved as I climbed the stairs. At the top, moonlight shone through a window in the roof above my head. The door to Crenshaw's apartment was right in front of me. I pushed on the button to the right of the door and heard a bell ring on the other side. The sound was followed by total silence. But no, wait a minute, there was something. I pressed my ear to the door and listened.

I can only describe what I heard as a faint scratching sound. It came and went, but when it came it was quick and desperate, almost as if something was trapped somewhere. I turned the handle of the door. As I'd expected, it was locked. The noise of the turning handle was followed by increased scratching. I suddenly remembered what Holmes had said about Crenshaw having a kitten. If he was right, maybe the animal was trapped somewhere in the apartment. I decided to see if there was another way in from the back of the house.

I walked around the side of the house and into the back garden. There was a gate at the far end which opened onto the path that Holmes and I had walked down two nights before. I looked back at the house. A set of iron stairs for use in case of fire led from the ground to the upper floor. I climbed to the top, found a door, and turned the handle. The door opened and I stepped into Crenshaw's apartment. I appeared to be in a large living room, almost the width of the house. At first, everything seemed to be in order, but as I walked past the first of two armchairs, I noticed a glass lying on its side on the floor. From the smell, I knew that it had contained whisky, which had now soaked into the carpet. I was just thinking this a little strange when I heard the scratching sound again. This time it was louder and came from the next room, to the front of the house. I followed the sound into a hallway. The door to Crenshaw's kitchen stood open on my left. I heard the sound again, this time directly above my head. I looked up and saw a square opening in the ceiling. It had a wooden cover which led into the attic. The kitten, if that's what it was, had obviously got trapped in there somehow. I looked around the hallway and found a stepladder★ in a cupboard beside the front door. I placed it beneath the opening and climbed to the top. I pushed on the cover and almost fell off the ladder as a terrified kitten landed on my shoulder and ran off into the night.

I was about to close the cover when something made me stop. It was a smell, the smell of whisky and something far more unpleasant. I pushed the cover open and lifted myself into the space beyond. As I did so, my right arm touched something hard. I took out a box of matches from my pocket and struck one. The flame lit up a shoe. It was attached to a dead man's leg.

I had no doubt the man was Crenshaw. His body lay in a strange position across the floor. His eyes were open and a rough, purple mark circled his neck. I knew at once that he was dead.

I was so shocked I forgot about the match. I dropped it with a cry of pain and was immediately thrown into complete darkness. Slowly and carefully, I climbed back down the stepladder.

I knew I had to call the police, but I hadn't noticed a phone in Crenshaw's apartment. The nearest one was at McCray's so I would have to go there. I left the way I'd come in, ran through the back gate, along the path, and into McCray's back garden.

Questions burned in my mind as I ran. Why had Crenshaw been killed? And where? In the living-room where I'd found the whisky glass, or in the attic? If the answer was the living-room, the murderer must be very strong to carry a dead body into the attic, a difficult job even with a small man like Crenshaw. I didn't need to ask why the body had been put there – obviously to delay discovery. The murderer probably hadn't noticed the kitten following its master into the attic. If it hadn't been for this small mistake, I would never have found the body.

As soon as I reached McCray's I saw that he was not alone. A light was burning in his study, where he sat at the table with Chief Inspector Carson and Amelia Finch. I wouldn't need a telephone after all.

I banged on the window. The people inside looked round in alarm. Amelia let me in through the back door. I went up to Carson, who was standing behind her, and told him what I'd found. He looked annoyed, probably because Crenshaw's murder would immediately weaken his case against Warman.

He went to McCray's study and called the police station for support. McCray sat in his wheelchair looking angry and shocked.

The police arrived within minutes. Carson said that he and I must accompany them to Crenshaw's apartment. He told Amelia she could go home after she'd given McCray any help he needed. He would speak to Mr McCray in the morning.

Before I left, McCray told me that the services of Holmes and myself were no longer required: the police would be handling everything from now on. He thanked me for the work we'd done, although he was clearly annoyed when I told him that Holmes had left Oxford. Accommodation at the Randolph had been arranged until Monday. A cheque for our services would be delivered to the reception desk that morning.

He then turned to Carson. "I heard from our family nurse in Scotland that my father is not expected to live more than a few days. I would like to go back to the family home early tomorrow to say my final goodbyes – if I'm not too late."

"Of course, sir," Carson replied. "Will you be able to manage?"

"I can easily arrange all the help I'll need, thank you," McCray replied.

"Very well, sir." Carson said. "I'll need the address of where you'll be staying, of course, and a telephone number if there is one."

McCray wrote the information down on a card and gave it to Carson. The inspector put it in his pocket then turned to me. "Let's go, Doctor."

Chapter 13

Into the Night

CD3 4

I didn't sleep at all that night. After accompanying Carson to the murder scene, I was forced to wait on a chair in the hallway outside Crenshaw's apartment while the police took photographs, put evidence in bags, and checked for fingerprints. The police pathologist* arrived and examined the body. I had no idea what his conclusions were, or if he even had any. I wondered about the time of death, of course, but Carson would give nothing away. Eventually, Crenshaw's body was removed and Carson asked me to accompany him to the police station to make a statement. He was obviously annoyed that his case against Jack Warman was growing weaker by the minute. I'd seen the manner of Crenshaw's death for myself. He'd died in more or less the same way as Annie Lawson: strangled by someone of considerable strength. There was almost no possibility that two different people had committed the murders.

I felt sure I knew who the real murderer was. It was the watcher who had followed Holmes and me through the park the first day we arrived in Oxford; the same figure in black I had seen through the mist that same night; and the man James Parker had seen watching Eleanor in the King's Arms. The proof was in the way Eleanor had reacted when she saw him later in Turl Street – terrified. The only thing that puzzled me was the identity of Eleanor's lover. I wondered how she had kept the affair secret from everyone she knew – with the possible exception of Annie.

I also didn't know the actual identity of the murderer,

of course. I couldn't even describe him very well. I tried to mention all this to Carson at the murder scene, but after he'd got me to explain how I'd found Crenshaw's body, he was too busy directing operations to pay me much attention.

It was only once we arrived at the police station that he listened to what I had to say. I told him all I knew. He became angry and demanded to know why I hadn't mentioned seeing the man in black before. I told him it was because I had assumed there was no point, because Warman had been arrested and charged so the investigation was over.

This did little to calm the inspector down. He told me to write a full report of everything I'd witnessed since arriving in Oxford. I could have refused, but I thought it would be better to cooperate.

I finished just as the sun was rising. Carson read through the report, had me sign it, and told a police officer to drive me back to the hotel. I was exhausted, and as soon as I got to my room I closed the curtains and went to bed.

I woke up late in the afternoon. I was hungry, so I got dressed and went downstairs to get a sandwich. After I'd eaten, I left the hotel and walked through the city centre. I could think of nothing more useful to do. The police were in control, McCray had left for Scotland, and the involvement of Holmes and myself had ended. I thought of returning to Baker Street but decided not to, since Holmes expected me to wait in Oxford until his return. This was one of our adventures I wouldn't be writing about, I thought to myself. For one thing, there was nothing to call it: 'Unfinished Mystery'? 'A Case With No End'? 'Unanswered Questions'? No one would want to read an account with such a disappointing title.

It was Sunday and the bells of Oxford's churches were ringing. They made a hopeful, calming sound – in strong contrast to the terrible events of the last four days. I tried to focus on pleasant things and was soon enjoying my walk through the older parts of the city.

At eight o'clock I began to make my way back to the hotel. It wasn't long before my calm mood was disturbed by questions I couldn't answer. Was the murderer one of the people on the list that Holmes had asked for? I hadn't met most of the people whose names Amelia Finch had given me, but even so, none of them seemed to be a likely murder suspect – except Warman, who now appeared to be innocent. There was also Holmes' odd point that the position of Crenshaw's flat in relation to 12 Allenby Road was 'interesting'. What on earth had he meant by that? And what did he expect me to do about it? Whatever it was, it was too late; Crenshaw was dead.

Then there was Holmes' description of my account as being 'almost entirely wrong'. I couldn't believe that. Had he been joking? If so, for what purpose? And did it have anything to do with his sudden disappearance? Where had he gone anyway? And why hadn't he told me?

I forced these questions out of my head. They were getting me nowhere. Tomorrow, I would take the train back to London, regardless of whether Holmes had returned by then or not. In the meantime, I would enjoy a final, pleasant dinner at the Randolph Hotel and get a good night's sleep.

I was right about the dinner, but wrong about the sleep.

Chapter 14

CD3 5

Otmoor

I was about to get undressed for bed when I heard the sound of someone running along the passage outside my room. They stopped and knocked loudly on the door. I opened it to find Holmes facing me, breathing heavily and covered in sweat.

"Put your coat on, Watson. We don't have much time."

"Time for what, Holmes? We're not on the case anymore. And where on earth have you been?"

Holmes ignored the questions, caught hold of my shoulders and looked me in the eyes. "Just listen. We need to get to Robert Lawson's as quickly as possible."

"Why?"

"We need two horses. We're going for a ride. To save a life, if we're not too late! It's Sunday night and there seem to be no cabs around – I had to run here from the station; so we'll have to get to Lawson's on foot. And bring your gun. We'll definitely need it." Before I had a chance to reply, Holmes was gone. I grabbed my coat and gun, and followed him down the stairs.

We ran all the way to the footbridge over the river Cherwell. Halfway across, I stopped for a moment to get my breath back. "Carry on, Holmes," I gasped, "I'll catch you up."

"No, it's better that we stay together."

"So perhaps you can tell me what on earth's happening?"

"Briefly. Eleanor Taylor is in a cottage just beyond a little village called Noke. It's on the edge of Otmoor –

the place she used to go bird-watching with her father. The murderer of Annie Lawson and Douglas Crenshaw now has that information. If it wasn't for you, Eleanor would be dead already."

"Me? What did I do?"

"You found Crenshaw's body. It delayed the murderer."

"How? And how do you know all this?"

"Remember I said your account was wrong?" I nodded. "I admit I was exaggerating a little; many of the points you made were accurate. But your focus was completely wrong. I've just returned from Oban, Scotland, which is where the answer to this mystery lies – not here in Oxford. I'll explain more later. Are you ready to continue?"

"Of course," I replied. I needed more time to understand the importance of this new information, but time was the one thing we didn't have.

"Then let's go."

The moon was fairly bright, making the footpath easy to follow. We reached Marston and ran up the track to Lawson's stables. The cottage behind was dark. I guessed Lawson was asleep.

Holmes tried the stable doors: locked. He ran up to the cottage and banged loudly on the front door. "Mr Lawson! Open up!"

A light went on above our heads, a window opened, and Lawson's face appeared. He was holding a torch and shining it in our faces. "Who is it?" he yelled.

Holmes put a hand over his eyes and replied, "Sherlock Holmes and Dr Watson, sir. We need two horses, immediately. It's a matter of life and death, but there's no time to explain. We'll return them by morning."

Lawson looked shocked, but reached to one side and threw down a set of keys.

"Take the two at the end, on the right. You'll find saddles* by the door. I'll be down in a moment."

Holmes had caught the keys and was already running back to the stables. Lawson arrived as we were saddling the horses. The urgency of the situation was obvious, and apart from asking if we'd found Eleanor Taylor – to which Holmes replied 'yes' – he asked no further questions.

Within minutes, we were ready to leave.

"Good luck!" Lawson yelled as we rode away.

Holmes seemed to know exactly where he was going. I followed his shape in the moonlight, through woodland and across streams, fields, and farms.

We rode five or six miles and reached Noke about thirty minutes later. The moon was now covered in cloud, but I could see that the village was very small; it had no more than a few cottages and an old church. We continued along its single main street and into what looked like open country covered in bands of silvery-grey mist. A dull light shone in the distance. As we rode closer, I saw that it came from the window of a small cottage directly ahead of us. The dark waters of Otmoor lay beyond.

The front door of the cottage was open. This was a bad sign. We quickly tied up the horses and went inside.

The cottage was a mess. It looked as if a fight had taken place. A chair was lying on its side, there was broken glass all over the floor, and through the back door ran a trail of blood.

"My God, Holmes. We're too late!"

"Shh, Watson. Listen."

Suddenly, I heard a scream coming from the direction of Otmoor. Holmes rushed out of the back door. "Leave the horses, Watson. We'll be better on foot." I pulled out my gun and followed.

Once outside, we could hear the sound of someone running through water. A gun fired. It was followed by a woman's cry and a heavier sound, as if whoever it was had fallen into the water. I felt sure it was Eleanor, and it sounded as if she'd been hit. I did the only thing I could think of to stop the killer from firing at Eleanor again: I raised my own gun and fired it into the air.

My shot was followed by a sinister silence. Holmes and I both moved forward through the mist. I noticed that the ground beneath our feet was becoming wetter. Every now and then, the mist cleared and we saw pools of water, low bushes, and what looked like a raised path to our right. I was about to run towards it when Holmes yelled, "Get down!"

I dropped to the ground as a bullet* flew over our heads. I lay as still as I could, unsure of what to do next. Holmes began to move forward on his hands and knees, so I did the same. To my great relief the mist returned, and I felt safer knowing that we couldn't be seen. But we were now covered in mud and moving blindly in the dark. Luckily, we managed to reach the bank of the path, where we lay on our stomachs, waiting and listening. After a few moments, we heard the sound of someone moving through water again. It came from somewhere to our left. As we looked, the mist cleared and in the light of the moon, we finally saw the slim figure of Eleanor Taylor, rising above the water, with long hair reaching down to the middle of her back.

I was just thinking how fortunate it was that Eleanor hadn't been hit when the killer fired again. Eleanor screamed, grabbed her left arm, and fell into the water. She'd been hit. The shot hadn't killed her, but unless the mist returned or we reached the killer before he fired again, the next shot probably would.

The shot had come from behind one of the bushes ahead of us on the right. I fired my gun in that direction as Holmes raced into the water towards Eleanor. Behind the bushes, nothing moved. Had I been lucky and hit the killer? There was only one way to find out, so I raced after Holmes, trying to keep an eye on the bush at the same time. The mist returned and I lost sight of everything except Holmes, who was a little way ahead of me. I caught up with him and we moved forward together, aware that the water was getting deeper with every step.

We were just passing a bush when it happened. I sensed a sudden movement to my right and turned, but I was too late; I felt a sharp pain in my right hand and dropped my gun into the water. The dark and sinister shape of a large man appeared above us.

"Stop, or you're both dead," the man shouted. "Put your hands on your heads." Strangely, his voice sounded familiar. I was just thinking this when the mist cleared once more and I saw Eleanor, a few metres ahead of us, holding her left arm. The wound didn't look too serious, but that didn't matter: we were all dead now, anyway.

I turned and faced the killer. When I saw his face, I almost fell back in amazement. The man standing above us was none other than our employer, Mr James McCray.

McCray turned to Holmes. "You knew, didn't you?"

"Yes," Holmes replied. "My suspicions were confirmed

when I got to Oban. My mistake was in not going sooner, and not allowing for the characteristics of Otmoor."

My ability to understand any of this was less important than our situation, which was desperate. McCray was on dry land and was able to move freely; we, on the other hand, were stuck in muddy water. And he was the only one with a weapon. Neither Holmes nor I would be able to reach McCray before he killed us all. Even the weather was against us: the mist had cleared and the whole scene was sharply lit by the moonlight.

At that point, Eleanor spoke for the first time. "Please, Uncle. Let them go."

"That would be unwise," he replied. "So would waiting for the mist to return. You first, my dear." He gave an evil smile and began to raise the gun. I thought of trying to throw water in his face. It wouldn't work, but we had to do something. We were going to die anyway; better to go down fighting than do nothing. Holmes must have had the same thought because we both lowered our hands into the water at the same time. McCray just laughed, stepped backwards, and brought his gun level with Eleanor's head.

I have often tried to describe the sound that followed. The closest I've ever come is this: imagine a child trying to play a wind instrument for the first time. They blow into one end and all that's produced is a faint whistling sound and a rush of air.

That is all we heard; the sound was followed by total silence. What we saw was far more dramatic. McCray seemed to turn to stone, unable to move or speak. His mouth stayed open in surprise. He fell, slowly, and dropped into the water with a great crash, like a block of stone. Once the water had settled, I saw a few bubbles rise to the surface. This continued for a few seconds as the mist returned. Then there was nothing.

We stood in silence for a moment. As we did so, I heard the sound of someone moving along the path towards us. I turned and saw the thin, dark figure of a man appear out of the mist. He was carrying what looked like a long stick. Again, I felt fear turn my blood to ice. It was the watcher in the park, the man Eleanor had been terrified of. Yet this man – whom I'd always thought of as the killer – had just saved our lives. Nothing made any sense.

Holmes turned to me and smiled. "Watson," he said. "Allow me to introduce you to Eleanor's father, Mr William Taylor."

CD3
6

Chapter 15

Back from the Dead

We were back at the cottage, sitting around a large fire. I hadn't allowed my disbelief to challenge my duties as a doctor. Fortunately, the wound to Eleanor's arm was minor: the bullet from McCray's gun had only caught the side of her upper arm. I cleaned the wound and wrapped it in a cotton bandage. This would be enough until we could get her to hospital in the morning.

McCray was dead, Holmes informed me. He'd been killed almost instantly by a deadly Amazonian poison, carried by a dart fired from a blowpipe.

William Taylor, the man responsible for McCray's death, started to explain the background to a mystery I was slowly beginning to understand.

"I never really knew James McCray," William began. "Only from the stories Alice told me. He'd always been jealous of his sister. That wasn't entirely his fault. Lord McCray's wife had died giving birth to James, and because of this Lord McCray was always cold towards his son. James grew bitter. He fought with his sister, failed at school, and, as he grew older, wasted money on drinking and playing cards. This only made Lord McCray favour Alice even more, leading to the consequences Mr Holmes discovered in Scotland."

"From some of the family's former servants," Holmes added. "I just had to decide what was true and what wasn't."

"But why did you decide to go there in the first place?" I asked.

Holmes looked at me and smiled. "McCray's act as a poor invalid wasn't entirely convincing, Watson. Although he wore a blanket over his legs, I could see they were thick and strong. The muscles of someone whose lower body is inactive would be thin and weak. There was also the movement of an active man in the legs, particularly when McCray tried to fake* emotion, for example, when he pretended to be angry with my suggestion that Eleanor had a lover. You may remember that I didn't sit down during the first part of the interview. This gave me the opportunity to observe these things. I was already suspicious, you see. Crenshaw's remark that McCray thought Eleanor had been taken against her will didn't make much sense, since we saw no trace of violence when we examined her college rooms. There was also McCray's 'feeling' that Eleanor had been contacted by someone. These were all the words and actions of a man who needed somebody like me to do all the physical work of finding Eleanor while he continued to act the part of an invalid*. In the meantime, he made it very clear that anything you or I found out, Watson, should only go to him, and to no one else. This would give him the opportunity to complete his plan. But I couldn't be sure of any of this. The watcher in the park confused me and I began to share your opinion, Watson, that he was the murderer. If that was the case, then perhaps McCray's illness was real – at least in mind if not in body. In other words, he was able to exercise his legs lying down, but had convinced himself he was unable to walk. It was only in Scotland that I was able to confirm my first suspicions. I also discovered who else was involved."

At this point, Eleanor spoke. "It was Lorna Stuart, wasn't it?"

"Yes," Holmes replied. "She and James had begun an affair shortly before your mother died."

"Was murdered, you mean," William said, bitterly.

"Yes, but that's impossible to prove," Holmes replied. "Lorna Stuart is a dangerous woman – attractive, clever, and cynical. She is the type of woman who has power over men and uses it to her advantage. Her husband, Dr Hamish Stuart, would do almost anything for her. When Alice went up to Oban on that final visit and fell ill, Lorna convinced him that she and James would be able to look after her. They didn't, of course. I believe they did everything they could to make your mother's illness worse. Lord McCray had already left for Edinburgh and I found out that James kept all the servants away from Alice's rooms soon after she fell ill."

"Yes, but not before she managed to give one of them a letter," William said. "She knew what was happening and wrote asking me to come and rescue her. By that time she was so sick she could hardly move. I didn't get her letter until six years later."

"In Brazil?" I asked.

"Right. The expedition I was on left from Manaus, the main city on the Amazon River. Mail from Scotland arrived soon after we'd left. The attack on the expedition was a tragic mistake. We had moored★ our boat along the river where its remains were later found. We were having a meal around a fire on the riverbank that night when a group of tribesmen arrived. They suddenly appeared out of the forest. Unfortunately, one of our men panicked, thinking we were about to be attacked. Before I could stop him, he had fired his gun and killed one of the tribesmen. Furious, I knocked the gun out of his hand and threw it into the river. But it was too late, of course. The tribe attacked, an arrow hit my left shoulder, and I turned and ran into the forest. The wound was not fatal but I was losing blood. I don't know how far I ran but eventually I could go no further and fell to the ground, unconscious★. When I woke up, I was lying under a tree. A native woman was leaning over me, cleaning the wound. She had removed the arrow but I was very ill with a fever★. Eventually, I was taken back to her tribe deep in the rainforest. It was a different tribe from the one that had attacked us. Luckily, I could speak some of their language and was able to communicate with them at a simple level.

"Anyway, whatever sickness I had affected the skin of my face. It turned dark and was covered in sores★. They gradually disappeared, but as you can see, they have left their mark. The woman who saved me was called Yanomi. She nursed me through the illness and we…" He glanced at Eleanor and seemed unwilling to continue.

She moved closer and pressed his hand. "Don't worry," she said. "I understand." She turned to us. "My father feels guilty," she said. "But there's no need. What he is trying to say is that he stayed with the tribe and Yanomi became like a second wife to him. I understand how that happened: he was lonely, thousands of miles from England; he'd lost everything apart from the clothes he was wearing. He was grateful to Yanomi. She had saved his life and brought some meaning back into it…"

"Yes," William interrupted, "and I was also keen to live with the tribe – for a while at least. There was so much I wanted to learn. And with my medical knowledge, I was able to help them, too. In the end, I lost all sense of time. I learned to hunt and make weapons, medicines, and poisons. Yanomi and I had a child, a boy called Tari. Shortly afterwards, Yanomi died. I was terribly upset and decided to leave the tribe, promising Tari that I would return one day. After gathering together everything that might be useful – mainly weapons, medicines, and poisons – I made my way back to the Amazon River. I soon found a boat going to Manaus and arrived in the city about one month later. I met an old friend of mine in the port*. I had changed so much he didn't recognise me; he'd thought I was dead, and it took me a long time to convince him that I wasn't. He finally believed me and took me to a storeroom* in the port. Any mail that arrived without a sender's address was kept there. This included the letter that Alice had written almost six years before. I cannot describe the guilt and pain I felt when I read what she had to say. I realised at once that James McCray wanted to inherit* everything his father had. This meant that Eleanor was in great danger. I was too late to save Alice but I might not be too late to rescue my daughter.

"It was to my advantage if James still believed I was dead. So I told my friend to say nothing and worked my way back to England on boats going to Belem. From there, I went to Lisbon and finally arrived in Southampton in late summer."

"You could have been too late," I said. "I can't see why McCray waited so long before he tried to kill Eleanor."

"Because of Lord McCray," said Holmes. "If anything happened to Eleanor while he was alive, James would be blamed and most probably disinherited*. Sadly, Lord McCray is no longer able to understand even the simplest information. This left James McCray free to act."

"Yes, I see." I turned back to William and asked, "How did you contact Eleanor?"

Eleanor answered for him. "In the only way that he knew I could be sure it was him. This cottage belongs to Professor Morley, but my father had a key so he could use it whenever he wanted. When I was a child, my father brought me here to watch the birds. I always loved that. He used to draw pictures of birds in flight in my diary, one for each of the days that we planned to stay here. It was clever, because if you turned the picture up the other way it looked like a 'W' – the first letter of my father's name. The first mail I received from my father contained one of those pictures. I knew for sure, then, that he was alive. You probably know everything that happened next."

"Why couldn't you have just gone to the college and told them who you were?" I asked.

William shook his head. "Impossible. My sickness and experiences in the Amazon had changed my appearance completely. I had no papers, nothing to prove who I was. Even Eleanor's word might not be enough. Remember that McCray was her legal guardian. Until I could prove beyond doubt that I was William Taylor, he would still be in control. If I had simply reported him to the police, he would have denied everything. Alice's letter was no proof. He would have described it as the work of a sick sister who had always hated him. In any case, I wanted to kill McCray. Anything less would still be a threat to Eleanor. But in the end, he almost killed me."

"So instead, you followed your daughter during her trips into town," Holmes said. "You wanted to find out what her routines were, who she knew, and how easy or difficult it would be for her to escape during the day – almost impossible, because she was always accompanied. Then, after making contact by letter, you arranged to meet her in St Giles' Church."

"That's right," Eleanor replied. "It was the Sunday of the week before I disappeared. I arranged for Douglas Crenshaw to call for me at the college and take me there."

"So Crenshaw knew you were meeting your father?"

Eleanor laughed. "Of course not. I had simply told him that I needed to pray, alone, for God to give me strength during my final year at university. Crenshaw was not a man who asked questions. He did exactly as he was told. It was still a risk, but not a big one if you knew Crenshaw as well as I did."

"Was there a special reason for meeting in the church?"

I asked.

"Yes," she replied. "My father wanted to tell me of the plan for my escape and that the clothing I needed would be at the post office the following afternoon. He held me in his arms, told me to be brave, and then I left."

"But what about James Parker?" I interrupted. "He told us that when you saw your father in Turl Street one day, you were terrified."

"Yes, but not of my father – we had already made contact by then. I was terrified of my uncle, who happened to appear at the same time. I didn't want him to see my father."

"So what does Crenshaw have to do with all this?" I asked Holmes. "You said he felt fear, not guilt. So what was he so afraid of?"

"I can't be sure, Watson," Holmes replied. "But I believe that shortly before Crenshaw came to London to see us, he saw something in 12 Allenby Road from the back window of his apartment. In the summer, the back of McCray's house is hidden behind the leaves of the trees. At this time of year, however, there are no leaves. I believe that the afternoon before he came down to London, he saw McCray walking around like any other healthy person. He was shocked and didn't know what to do. Suddenly, the whole situation seemed suspicious. But he was not a confident man; he knew that if he said anything, McCray would deny it. Crenshaw might lose his job as a consequence, and with it a safe future as a married man. However, following Annie's death, he became more of a threat to McCray, who had probably grown suspicious by then anyway. McCray decided to take no chances. He went round to Crenshaw's, took him by surprise, murdered him, and hid his body in the attic. This was after he'd killed Annie, of course. When he realised that Annie had Eleanor's parcel and a clue to where she was hiding, he left his house in the early hours of Friday morning, waited for her to appear along the path that leads to the footbridge over the Cherwell and murdered her on the far side of the river. He took the empty parcel and saw the bird drawings. Because their meaning was common knowledge in the family, he knew not only what they meant, but also who Eleanor was with, and where they were hiding. He planned to come to this cottage and kill both William and Eleanor. As I said earlier, Watson, if it wasn't for you and that kitten, he might have succeeded. But you found Crenshaw's body and the police were called. They arrived at McCray's and he was forced to postpone the plan.

"Later that night, I believe he got rid of his wheelchair. It's probably lying at the bottom of the Cherwell now. He had told Carson earlier that he had to go to Scotland to visit his dying father – a lie, of course. He planned to come here the following night and complete his evil plan."

"He took me by surprise," William said. "I had gone out to get some wood for the fire. As I bent down, McCray hit me on the back of the head with the handle of his gun and knocked me out. He could have shot me, but he wanted to take Eleanor by surprise."

"In the end, his plan didn't quite work," Eleanor said. "I was in the hall, on my way to the kitchen, when McCray appeared at the back door. I screamed and ran out of the front door and onto the moor*. Because of the mist, I was able to avoid him for some time."

"When McCray hit me," William said, "I was wearing a thick woollen hat. It protected me from the full force of the blow and I must have woken up just before you and Dr Watson arrived. I heard Eleanor scream, ran up to the room where I keep my weapons, and went out onto the moor. I knew what was happening but had to wait for the mist to clear before I could see McCray clearly enough to hit him with the dart. I don't think I've ever felt so thankful as when I saw his body drop into the water."

We talked through the night. As the sun was rising, we rode the horses back to Marston, William and his daughter on one horse, Holmes and I on the other. As we approached the village I saw the towers of Oxford rising up through the mist. The city lay beneath. Someone famous had once described the view as 'sad'.

At that moment, I couldn't have agreed with them more.

CD3 7

Epilogue

Holmes and I returned to London on Tuesday morning. The previous evening, we had accompanied William Taylor to the hospital where Eleanor was recovering from the injury to her arm. She told us that she had received a visit from her Aunt Edith and Miss Blake. They were both sympathetic, and horrified by what had happened. Miss Blake had assured Eleanor that she would be welcomed back to college once she felt well enough to return. Edith had described the safe return of both her brother and her niece as one of the happiest moments of her life. William would now take possession of the family home, and Eleanor would spend her weekends and holidays there until she finished her studies.

Holmes expressed his good wishes to Eleanor, and said a special thank you to William, who had saved all our lives. But he quickly grew tired of this display of gratitude and happiness. His mind was already in another place, and as soon as it was polite to do so, we made our excuses and left.

On the train back to London, I sat staring out of the window, wondering at the emotions of the people involved in what I now referred to as the 'Oxford Murders'.

How did Eleanor feel about having a half-brother deep in the Amazon Rainforest? Would her father want to return one day, taking her with him? Would Robert Lawson ever recover from the loss of his daughter? What would happen between Eleanor and James Parker? And how would Lorna Stuart react to the death of James McCray?

None of these questions bothered Holmes in the least. For him, the case was over. Another problem solved. The nightmare of 'normal' life was returning. He marked it with restless energy and frequent trips to the train's restaurant bar. I hoped and prayed that a new case would be waiting for him in the near future. Either that, or something truly amazing, like falling in…

No, 'love' was not a word that easily came to mind when I thought of Sherlock Holmes.

EXERCISES

A Comprehension

Prologue – Chapter 3

1 What was 'mysterious' about Eleanor Taylor's disappearance?

2 Why did Dr Watson think Holmes wanted to catch an earlier train to Oxford?

3 Sherlock Holmes described Douglas Crenshaw as a 'liar'? Why?

4 Which three places did Holmes think were connected to Eleanor's disappearance?

5 How did Dr Watson feel as he walked through the University Parks?

Chapters 4 – 6

6 Which of the possible reasons Holmes gave for Eleanor's disappearance made James McCray angry?

7 According to James McCray, when was the last time he saw Eleanor?

8 Who shared rooms with Eleanor Taylor?

9 Name all the people that were in the kitchen when Holmes questioned Annie.

10 How did Dr Hamish Stuart die?

Chapters 7 – 9

11 Why did Dr Watson say he felt glad that he was 'educated in Edinburgh' rather than Oxford?

12 What did Holmes and Watson hear when they were in Eleanor's rooms?

13 *'Now I will have to tell James'*. Who said this and why?

14 What did Sherlock Holmes say was the reason that Eleanor gave everything she was wearing on the day she disappeared to Annie?

15 Why do you think Holmes describes Watson's account as 'almost entirely wrong'? Give your ideas and opinion.

Chapters 10 – 12

16 Give three reasons why the policeman, Chief Inspector Carson, was annoyed at Sherlock Holmes and Dr Watson.

17 Who was Jack Warman and how did Holmes and Watson know him?

18 What did Watson find strange about the letter he received from Holmes?

19 Of the people that visited James McCray in the past month, how many did Amelia Finch name? What are their names?

20 What was the reason Watson gave for the killer putting his victim's body in the attic?

Chapters 13 – Epilogue

21 *'I felt sure I knew who the real murderer was,'* said Watson early in Chapter 13. Who was the person Watson was thinking of?

22 How did Watson lose his gun?

23 One person died in Chapter 14. How were they killed?

24 Where did Sherlock Holmes discover the answer to the mystery?

25 What did Sherlock Holmes think was Douglas Crenshaw's secret?

B Working with Language

Chapters 1 – 5

1 Which of the following adjectives do not describe Douglas Crenshaw?

strong nervous confident fearless frightened secretive

2 Look at this example of a third conditional sentence and make more sentences using the prompts below.

Example: prompt: If Sherlock Holmes/be home/Douglas Crenshaw/not/call
full sentence: 'If Sherlock Holmes had been at home, Douglas Crenshaw wouldn't have called.'

a If Dr Watson/phone/McCray/he/knew/come.

b If it hadn't/be misty/University Park/have seem/less frightening.

c If Annie Lawson hadn't/arrive/McCray's/Holmes/not know about the parcel.

d If McCray hadn't/ give Holmes/ photograph/ he / not know what Eleanor looked like.

3 **Complete the following sentences with the correct form of the verbs in brackets.**

a Holmes realised that someone (watch) them in the park.

b Watson (be) surprised when Holmes didn't visit the Pitt Rivers Museum.

c Leaving Beaufort Hall alone (be / not / allow).

d James McCray (have) already (arrange) an interview with Miss Blake.

Chapters 6 – 10

4 **Match the formal verb in brackets on the left with its phrasal verb form on the right.**

a	Eleanor Taylor (travelled) to Oban to visit her grandfather.	**i)**	passed over
b	Watson saw a dark figure and (held) Holmes arm.	**ii)**	looked around
c	Holmes (gave) Watson the newspaper he'd been reading.	**iii)**	caught hold of
d	Holmes (examined) Eleanor's rooms.	**iv)**	went up to

5 **Give the adjective forms for the following nouns:**

urgency secret anxiety shadow attention coincidence mystery ambition interference curiosity trust

Chapters 11 – 15

6 Choose the correct preposition to complete each of the following sentences:

about under onto down between off

a Watson found a newspaper ______________ Annie's mattress.

b The garden gate opened ______________ a path ______________ the houses.

c Watson almost fell ______________ the ladder.

d Watson wondered ______________ the time of death.

e The information didn't calm the inspector ______________.

7 Arrange the following words or phrases into three categories, Brazil, Oxford, or Oban, according to which of these places they have a connection to in the story:

blowpipe servant expedition cottage 'an affair'
kitten boat nurse dart tribe 'post office'
'playing cards' church arrow

C Activities

1 Write an account of what might have happened if William Taylor had received his wife's letter before he left for Brazil.

2 Choose any three of the main characters from the story. Then choose one of the illustrations in the book and write a scene for a play involving all three characters in the illustration you have chosen.

3 Write the story that might have appeared in an Oxford newspaper following William Taylor's return from Brazil.

GLOSSARY

abduct *(v)* to take someone away by force

accompany *(v)* to go somewhere with someone as their companion

alibi *(n)* something that proves a person was in a different place from where a crime happened

anthropologist *(n)* someone who studies people, societies and their culture

aristocrat *(n)* someone who has a title and a high position in society

blanket *(n)* a large piece of cloth people put over their body to keep warm, usually in bed

blowpipe *(n)* a long hollow pipe used for blowing poisonous darts

bullet *(n)* a small metal object which is fired from a gun

cart *(n)* a wooden vehicle with two or four wheels, usually pulled by a horse

chemistry *(n)* the scientific study of materials and the way they react with each other

coal *(n)* black rock taken from under the ground and used as fuel

coalman *(n)* a person who delivers coal

coat hanger *(n)* a triangular-shaped object used for hanging clothes in a wardrobe

compartment *(n)* a small room on a train with seats for passengers

confused *(adj)* to find something difficult to understand because it is complicated or unclear

dart *(n)* a small object with a sharp point which sticks into things when it is thrown or blown

disabled *(adj)* someone who can't move about easily because of illness or injury

disinherit *(v)* to stop someone from receiving money or property after a person's death by changing a legal document

drainpipe *(n)* a long pipe at the side of a building through which water travels from the roof to the ground

expedition *(n)* an organised journey made by a group of people, often for a scientific purpose

fake *(v)* to fake something is to pretend that something happened, or is happening, when it didn't

fever *(n)* you have a fever when your blood is hotter than it should be because of an illness

fingerprints *(n)* the pattern made by someone's fingers on an object or surface they've touched

fireworks *(n)* objects that burn with a coloured flame and move, make a loud noise, or fly into the air when they are lit

graveyard *(n)* an area of land, usually next to a church, where dead bodies are buried

guardian *(n)* someone who is legally responsible for another person, especially a child

housekeeper *(n)* someone who cleans and looks after someone else's house

inherit *(v)* to be given money or property by someone after they die

marshland *(n)* an area of land which is very soft and wet

microscope *(n)* a scientific instrument which makes small objects look bigger

milkman *(n)* a person who delivers milk

moor *(n)* a moor is an area of wild, lonely, open land with almost no trees

moored *(adj)* a boat is moored when it is tied to something on land to stop it moving

overslept *(v)* to have slept longer than you wanted to

pathologist *(n)* a qualified person in the police service who examines a body to find out the cause of death

port *(n)* a town by the sea or a river where ships deliver goods or passengers

porter *(n)* someone who looks after a building and guards its entrance

pray *(v)* to speak to a god you believe in to ask for help

remains *(n)* the parts that are left of something after it's been destroyed, or someone after they are dead

saddle *(n)* a leather seat which goes on a horse's back

sinister *(adj)* something that makes you afraid because it is evil or can harm you

skyline *(n)* the shape made by the tops of buildings seen against the sky

sores *(n)* sores are red marks on the skin caused by an illness

stable *(n)* a building for keeping large animals, usually horses, in

stepladder *(n)* a small ladder usually used inside a building for reaching high places

storeroom *(n)* a room used for storing things

strangle *(v)* to strangle someone is to squeeze their neck to stop them breathing until they are dead

stuffed *(adj)* a dead animal is 'stuffed' when the inside of its body is replaced with soft material so that it can be preserved and displayed in a public museum or private building

thistles *(n)* wild plants with prickly leaves which can hurt if they touch your skin

tribe *(n)* a group of people who share the same customs, language and land

unconscious *(adj)* unable to move, see, or notice things, often because of a blow or injury to the back of the head

warehouse *(n)* a large building used for storing things

ANSWER KEY

A Comprehension

Chapter 1

1 No evidence of a crime; no reason for her to leave
2 So that Holmes could surprise Crenshaw
3 He believed that Crenshaw was deliberately avoiding him.
4 University Parks, Beaufort Hall, Pitt Rivers Museum
5 Lonely and afraid
6 That Eleanor made a lover's arrangement
7 Last Sunday evening
8 Helen Richards
9 Holmes, Annie, Watson, Amelia Finch, James McCray and Douglas Crenshaw
10 In a climbing accident
11 Because of the violent crimes in Oxford
12 A woman's scream
13 Millie Parker, she must tell her brother James that Eleanor had a secret lover
14 So that people would assume she was still wearing the clothes, which would make her more difficult to find
15 Students' own answers
16 i) He wanted to speak to Holmes and Watson earlier but they'd already left;
ii) They were investigating the case without reporting it to the police;
iii) They intended to carry on investigating.
17 Annie Lawson's boyfriend. Holmes and Watson knew him as the driver of the horse and cart they saw.
18 Holmes' mention of the back windows of Crenshaw's flat
19 Eleven people – Eleanor, Annie, Mr. Crenshaw, John Finch, Edith, Jack Warman, Jason Hicks, Helen Richards, Millie and James Parker

20 To delay its discovery

21 The man he saw in the University Parks on his first day in Oxford

22 By dropping it into the water on Otmoor

23 James McCray; he was killed by a poisoned dart, fired by William Taylor

24 In Oban, Scotland

25 That he knew James McCray was lying about his disability

B Working with Language

1 strong, confident, fearless

2 a) If Dr Watson had phoned, McCray would have known he was coming.

b) If it hadn't been misty, University Park would have seemed less frightening.

c) If Annie Lawson hadn't arrived at McCray's, Holmes would not have known about the parcel.

d) If McCray hadn't given Holmes the photograph, he would not have known what Eleanor looked like.

3 a) was watching b) was c) was not allowed d) had; arranged

4 a) iv b) iii c) i d) ii

5 urgent, secretive, anxious, shadowy, attentive, coincidental, mysterious, ambitious, interfering, curious, trusting

6 a) under b) onto; between c) off d) about e) down

7 Brazil – blowpipe, expedition, boat, dart, tribe, arrow

Oban – servant, nurse, 'playing cards', 'an affair'

Oxford – kitten, church, 'post office'

C Activities

Students' own answers